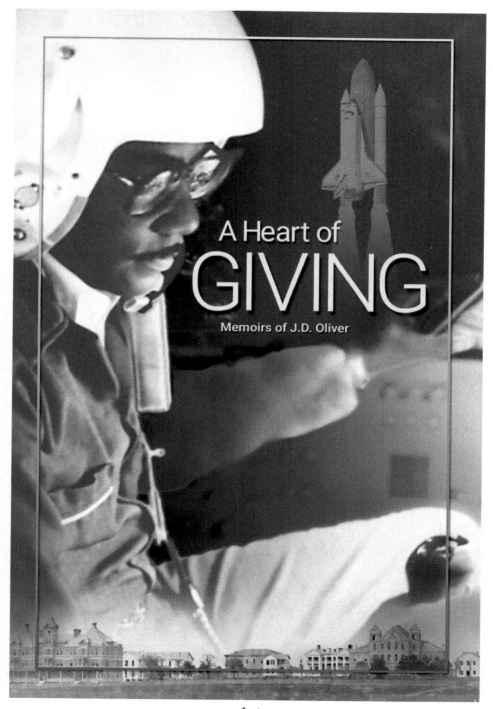

A Heart of
GIVING

Memoirs of J.D. Oliver

outskirts
press

Outskirts Press, Inc.
http://www.outskirtspress.com

Paperback ISBN: 978-1-9772-2680-8
Hardback ISBN: 978-1-9772-3143-7

Library of Congress Control Number: 2020912686

Cover Design © 2021 Neal Brooks. All rights reserved - used with permission.
Prairie View A&M University (circa 1876), J.D. in the F-16 fighter jet flight navigation control panel simulator © Author's collection, and the STS-1 Columbia space shuttle © NASA

Outskirts Press and the "OP" logo are trademarks belonging to Outskirts Press, Inc.

PRINTED IN THE UNITED STATES OF AMERICA

Table of Contents

Acknowledgments

As I reflect over my life, there are so many to whom I owe thanks. I am unable to acknowledge them all here, but without their support, guidance, and influence I would not have a story to tell.

I must first acknowledge my Heavenly Father, without whom I am nothing. His love, grace, mercy, forgiveness, and protection have allowed me to be where I am. Without Him, I would not have been able to write my memoir, share my life's story, and, hopefully, inspire others to do the same. It is through God's grace and mercy that I was able to build a computer science program to educate numerous students and launch their careers. The lyrics of Andraé Crouch's song "My Tribute" says it all—*To God be the glory for the things He has done.*

My parents, J.D., Sr. and Corrie Lee Oliver, gave their children all they had. It is through their love, examples, and teachings of Christian principles that I am who I am. Although they are not physically present, their spirits have always been with me as I worked to become who I am.

ii

The support of Aunt Callie was invaluable to my brother and me, instilling in us the importance of education and helping us achieve that goal. I know that she is smiling down on me, proud of what was accomplished.

The love of siblings can never be measured. We were a close-knit family, always protecting and supporting each other. My sister Gladys has always championed her older brothers – always in our corners, always there for us. I am forever grateful to her for continually encouraging me to complete my memoir.

Elnora Flewellen is like another sister to me. From the time we began working together at Lockheed in 1969, Elnora has been there to experience both good times and sad times with us. She helped provide research and review information for my memoir. Elnora, thank you for being who you are and for supporting me.

My church family is important to me. My sincerest appreciation to Pastor Emeritus William A. Lawson for his profound teachings over the years that have kept me rooted in my faith. I thank God for Senior Pastor Marcus D. Cosby, whose encouraging sermons reminds us that if God has given us a challenge, we must be obedient to His will and see it through to completion. Many thanks to our Family Group Bible Study and Sugar Land Bible Study Group for your collective encouragement. Your support has meant a lot!

My son Jay and I have a father-son bond that I will always cherish. As we grew older, we became closer. He is strongly rooted in family and has supported me unconditionally in all that I do. No matter where life has taken us, he has been there cheering me on—especially in the writing of my story. I can never say "thank you" enough to my son, but I sure can say "I love you!"

My story would not have been written were it not for my wife, Carolyne. I began gathering materials to write my memoir around 2012. As my challenges increased due to Parkinson's disease and my stamina for teaching diminished, I was no longer able to continue the effort. Carolyne picked up my project after her retirement in 2015 and became the driving force, never allowing me to give up. Somehow just saying "thank you" is not enough for her dedication and commitment to help get my story published. She has been there fifty plus years to love, support and encourage me in everything I do. So, I say, "I will always love you… not only for who you are, but for making a difference in my life."

Dedication

This book is dedicated to my twin brother, A.D.,
with whom I shared 80 years of life.
We supported one another throughout our lives.
I can hear his encouragement, as he would always ask,
"Where are you on your book? Have you completed it yet?"
I miss him greatly, but I have the comfort of knowing
he is looking down from heaven
and sharing in my joy
because the book is complete!

PROLOGUE

My father, J.D. Oliver Sr., was a visionary in so many ways. He was a strong advocate of education and felt it was the steppingstone to success. Although he did not have the opportunity to attend college, he achieved the highest level of education he could at the time—the eighth grade at the Antioch Common School in his community.

While his access to formal education was limited, he did not let that deter him from the thirst for education. He read a lot of books, read about world events, and talked to us about what was happening in the world. His favorites were the Bible and articles about political issues. He became a preacher, and, I might add, he was quite good with referencing the Bible and determining who would be the best politician to vote for. He would keep up with current events through two newspapers whenever he could get hold of them—the *Houston Post* and *Austin Statesman*, both weekly newspapers. He was a good speller, self-taught, and had beautiful handwriting.

He and his youngest sister, my aunt Callie, were dedicated to each other. Dad was a farmer and didn't earn a lot of money because times were pretty hard. However, he saw great potential in Callie. So, with his encouragement and financial support, she went to Prairie View A&M University, which was then called Prairie View Normal and Industrial College, located in Prairie View, Texas, about sixty miles from our home in Ledbetter. Callie was the first and only one of the siblings to go to college. She graduated from Prairie View with honors.

Later in life, at the age of forty, Dad fell in love with my mother, Corrie Lee Irving, who was twenty years younger. They married, lived in Ledbetter, and two years later, they were blessed with twin sons, me and A.D. Mom and Dad had six children within a fifteen-year span. I am the oldest with A.D., then Earl, Katharine, Gladys, and Mary Francis. Katharine died from pneumonia when she was two weeks old. Dad was forty-two when A.D. and I were born and fifty-seven when Mary Francis, our youngest sister, was born. The family later moved from Ledbetter to Dime Box, Texas.

Dad worked hard as a farmer to provide essentials such as food, clothing, and shelter, but did not earn enough to provide a college education for his children. When A.D. and I graduated from high school and were ready to go off to college, Aunt Callie remembered what my dad had done for her and decided to pay our tuition to Prairie View. She was teaching in Dallas at the time, but supported us by her example, encouragement, and funding. She never had children of her own, so we were the next best thing for her—thinking of us as her sons. Aunt Callie became invaluable in our lives from babies to adulthood. She would send us clothes and shoes when we were kids. A.D. and I reaped the benefit of what Dad had sowed in Aunt Callie.

As Mom and Dad grew older, they were living on a fixed income with a lot of health problems and medical bills. So, when my sister Gladys finished high school and was interested in going to Prairie View, Mom and Dad did not have any money for her schooling. I thought about how blessed A.D. and I were for having Aunt Callie pay our tuition. Now it was time for me to do a selfless act for my sister, who wanted to further her education, so I paid her tuition to Prairie View. Gladys, in turn, sent her three children to Prairie View, and they now have successful careers.

It all goes back to our self-sacrificing father, who sent his sister to college. I am pretty sure that Dad had no idea when he supported Callie's education that she would spiral around to help his sons, who helped his daughter, who helped his grandchildren attend and graduate from the same university. Nor did he have any idea that two of his grandchildren would come back to work and manage the family-owned land in Lee County—where it all began.

As I reflect on my life and professional career, I realize that Dad's strong support for education laid the foundation for my success.

Aunt Callie reinforced education by encouraging us to teach, constantly reminding us, "As long as there is a Black child, there will be a need for Black teachers." The seed for education and giving back was now rooted in me, and I knew that no matter what career path I took, whether it was working in the corporate world or teaching in public school or higher education, it was my responsibility to do all I could to make life better for others.

Dad and Mom did not have the opportunity to attend college, but I believe they both would have been incredible students. Nevertheless, they instilled in us a work ethic and an attitude to always do our best and look our best. They taught us to be thankful to God for allowing us to do well, and that we had a responsibility to give back.

Chapter 1

"We Have Liftoff..."

Spectators and the news media are gathered at Kennedy Space Center with all cameras focused on the spacecraft sitting atop its booster rocket. It is a clear day with a beautiful blue sky. The only cloud is an emission from the booster rocket on the ground as all systems are go for the flight. My family and I are glued to the television to watch the space flight, and we catch glimpses of the spectators at Kennedy. Never in my wildest dreams would I have thought that the math I learned from George Washington Edwards back at Fairview School in Dime Box, my education at Prairie View A&M University, and all the National Science Foundation (NSF) Math and Science Institutes A.D. and I attended would lead me to this point in my life.

Everyone at Mission Control checks and rechecks systems to make certain everything is working as programmed. You can see the anticipation on their faces as they work to ensure everything will go as scheduled. There is a countdown, and the retractable gantry backs away from the rocket—*10, 9, 8, 7, 6...*

I can't help thinking that the programming A.D., Elnora, Melvin, and I did is a significant part of this space mission—*5, 4, 3, 2, 1.* The cloud under the launch pad enlarges and the rocket rises.

We have liftoff!

The rocket pushes the attached spacecraft high into the sky, and within a few minutes, the booster rocket thrusts the spacecraft into its moon orbit. The booster falls back to the earth into the ocean, and ships head out to retrieve it so that it can be used again. Another successful liftoff!

Lockheed Electronics, where we worked, was only one of the many subcontractors at NASA Johnson Space Center in Houston, where all the research, programming, and testing of space flights occurred. NASA's control center, called Mission Control, where monitoring and communication with astronauts during flights took place, was also at the Johnson Space Center. Rockets were built at NASA-Michoud in New Orleans, an assembly facility on the border of Mississippi and Louisiana. NASA had several launch and landing sites, but Cape Canaveral at Kennedy Space Center in Florida was the primary location.

I often wondered why Houston was the site for Mission Control and not Florida, where the launches took place. But I soon learned that of the twenty-three possible sites for NASA to choose from to build its control center, Houston was chosen partly due to political reasons—the push from Lyndon Johnson to bring a major portion of the space program to Texas, and partly because of the opportunities and advantages of being near a large city. Access to 1,000 acres of land in the Clear Lake area near Houston and the availability of skilled labor and the manpower to build Mission Control were good reasons for NASA to say yes to Houston.

Like NASA, I had good reason to say yes to Houston. When I accepted the job offer from Lockheed Electronics at the Space Center in 1969, it gave me the opportunity to fulfill my dream of working in corporate. Although I did not know it at the time, this move led me to marriage and a family, and put me on the path to fulfill my responsibility to give back to my community.

Columbia Space Shuttle (STS-1) Launch
April 12, 1981 – I was a member of the Ascent Team, analyzing
and testing software for the shuttle launch. (NASA)

Chapter 2

Student Life at Prairie View

Experiences of J.D. and A.D. as
students at Prairie View and life
as young African American men in
the South in the late 1950s.

A.D. and I left home in September 1957 to attend Prairie View
A&M University, then known as Prairie View A&M College
and often referred to as Prairie View or PV. We didn't have a clue
about what to do or what to expect once we got there. Maybe it was
good that we didn't know, because when we arrived, one of the first
problems we ran into was with the dormitories.

We were assigned to Foster Hall and there were three of us in a
room—A.D., Paul Stiner, and me. It was the pits. The dorm was in
bad shape and poorly maintained. Bathrooms unkept, torn furniture, walls not painted. Conditions were horrible. The dorms were
once military barracks and they were not good enough for soldiers

anymore, so the government moved them to Prairie View. Parents would bring their children to the campus, and before they could move them into the dorms, they would have to get washing soap and clean out the place, scrub it down.

Paul's father complained and said he would not allow his son to stay in that room because it was so bad. After Paul's father had a conversation with the dean, the dean found a room at Woodruff Hall for Paul and the two of us. It was a better dormitory, decent living there, and we settled in. There was a bunkbed—A.D. had the bottom bunk, and I had the top. Stiner was on the single. Paul's father also wanted us to have a good meal now and then. He owned a barbecue business in Houston and when he would come to see Paul, he would bring us barbecue. Other people would ask for some of our food, but we weren't sharing. We had it pretty good.

Paul studied electrical engineering and had a tough schedule. He went to class, studied hard, and never got much rest. He was laid back and slept when he wasn't in class. A.D. and I decided to focus on industrial education as a major and mathematics as a minor. I took more math courses than A.D., don't know why. During our freshman year, A.D. and I would get up at seven o'clock in the morning and have breakfast in the dining hall. Standard menu—grits, eggs, sausage, hot cakes, coffee, juice.

Sometimes we cooked in the room, and sometimes we ate in the cafeteria in Hilliard Hall. The meal plan was a separate cost, paid by the semester in the cafeteria. Cooking in the room on a hot plate was not permitted, but we did it anyway. Hilliard Hall is still there, although renovated many times, and now houses the School of Communications.

Registration was challenging. A lot of time was spent filling out punch cards for each class. Our first class at Prairie View was drafting, part of the industrial education curriculum. We had a teacher named Professor Goode who taught basic courses like algebra and trigonometry. My favorite was calculus, taught by Dr. A.D. Stewart in my freshman and sophomore years. Other professors were Drs. S.R. Collins, Price, and McGee. I enjoyed computing—velocity and derivatives, increasing the power, and applications. Logic was also a favorite, but pure applications is what I enjoyed the most. Of course we had to take core courses such as English, speech, and government.

We had good professors and administrators—Professors Allen and C. L. Wilson, Dr. Alvin I. Thomas, Dr. J.L. Brown, Herbert Smith, and Dr. Ann Campbell, a professor who was chair of the English department. Dr. Thomas was dean of the College of Industrial Education, or general shop as it was called back then. He taught Freshman Orientation, but I didn't have any other classes with him. Later, he became president of the university. Wilson was dean of the College of Engineering. Engineering courses were not required for Industrial Education majors, but I took math courses with engineering students. I increased my mathematics skills with college algebra, trigonometry, differential and integral calculus, more algebra, and differential equations. I didn't struggle in any of those classes. I had my books to study from because Aunt Callie paid for those along with tuition. I did not go to the library much for reference because it was limited, so most of what I learned came from textbooks and professors.

Physical education was a required course, and we had ROTC (Reserve Officers' Training Corps). Every able-bodied male was required to take ROTC in his freshman and sophomore years. Then it was up to the student to continue in his junior and senior years. After the two-year requirement was met, ROTC was called Advanced Corps. Commitment to the Corps may be the reason so many Prairie View graduates became military generals.

Life on campus was okay. There was a big old building called the Rec Center where we would go and sit and talk, play cards, drink coffee and Cokes, eat a hamburger—that sort of thing. There weren't any Greek organizations on campus. We didn't know anything about them, but we had social clubs—The Barons, The Crescendos. I became a member of The Barons, and we would have get-togethers and dances. We went through an initiation and paid dues just like any other fraternal organizations. We were a fraternity without being Greek.

A.D., Paul, and I had girlfriends. We would do some solo dating and sometimes A.D. and I would double date. Prairie View was a dry county, and alcohol was prohibited on campus. We couldn't carry drinks to our Barons' parties, but some of the guys wanted it and managed to get it from somewhere. There was a nearby restaurant—Tory's—that served alcohol, but we weren't interested in drinking. Our Christian faith was part of the reason we didn't drink.

Ladies lived on one side of the campus, and we were on the other side, separated. They had their own dorm with a house mother who knew which young lady was going out with which young man. The ladies had to sign out of the dorm and stay on their side of campus. They couldn't go over to the boys' area, couldn't even walk over there. And we were not supposed to go to the ladies' side of the campus and just hang out. Some young ladies had jobs on campus. They worked at the dining hall or at the library. My sister worked at Evans Hall, the girls' dormitory, when she was a student. Some of the young ladies majored in Home Economics and spent a great deal of time in what was called the Home Ec building, learning to cook and sew. Their boyfriends really had it made because they benefitted from all that cooking and sewing.

When we were courting, we would go to movies in the gymnasium on Friday and Saturday nights at seven o'clock. We would meet the ladies at the dorm and escort them to the movie. We had to have them back by ten o'clock as that was their curfew. Some couples would sneak off, but that was hard to do because it was a small campus. Other than the movies on the weekend, or the Barons or Crescendos events, there wasn't much social life. The administration expected us to study the rest of the time.

We didn't leave campus often. Paul lived in Houston and his father would come and pick him up from time to time. We went with him to Houston once or twice, but A.D. and I hardly left Prairie View during the semester. We went to vespers, also known as chapel, on campus. It was like an interdenominational worship service and was required—every Sunday morning at 11 a.m.—lasting about an hour. We would get up, get breakfast, and go to vespers.

We would go home for Thanksgiving and Christmas. A.D. and I would put on our ROTC uniforms and start walking in hopes of catching a ride—hitchhiking. We'd walk a little while, and if we heard a car, jack up that thumb and people would pick us up and take us as far as they were going. That was a common means of travel and how we got home for the holidays. We did the same thing in reverse to get back to school after the holidays. Prairie View was totally segregated then, but white people never bothered us. They just left us alone. We didn't even encounter white folks going in and out of campus and didn't have any problems.

During our sophomore year, we lived in the dorm and ate out. This was possible because A.D. and I got a job with Coca-Cola. We serviced all the Coke machines on campus. We got the job through Dr. Alvin Thomas and a student by the name of Louis Morris. When Louis graduated, Whitney, the white man from Brenham, Texas, who delivered Coca-Cola and candy to the campus, asked Dr. Thomas if he knew anyone he could recommend to work the Coke machines. Dr. Thomas recommended my brother and me. We told Aunt Callie that we were the Coke guys, so she stopped sending pocket money and just paid tuition and books. She was impressed that A.D. and I were being industrious in terms of making our own money. It was probably a relief for her and gave her a chance to save money so she could buy property.

Everybody knew us because we were twins and the "Coke guys". Whitney would bring soda, candy, and cookies to campus. The soda was in large silver commercial cans. Students would insert a nickel, a cup dropped down, and Coke was dispensed into it. We would take empty cans out of the machine and replace them. We managed the cups, soda cans, and candy. Extra cups and candy were kept in the bottom of the machine in a locked storage bin.

If students got hungry, they could buy Baby Ruth, Snickers, peanuts, or cookies. When we entered the girls' dorms, we would say, "Man on the hall!" A.D. and I would go into the vending room and set up the machine so they could get Cokes. We also serviced the men's dorms, which was a lot easier because we could come and go without hesitating.

Whitney would come down to Prairie View when we had to take money out of the machine. Whitney emptied the coin bins, we would help him count, and then he would take the money. We would check each machine after class and service the machines every evening. If the machines were low on candy, we would put more in, and if the machines were broken, we would fix them. We would fill up those machines on the weekends, making sure there was plenty of candy, cookies, and Coke.

Commencement

When A.D. and I were in our junior and senior years and moved into advanced classes, we were doing just fine in math and science. As an Industrial Education major, I received a teaching certificate along with my degree. Prairie View had a regular commencement exercise, and there were about sixty of us who graduated in 1961. Dr. E. B. Evans was the president, and the ceremony wasn't long. Dr. Benjamin Mays, president of Morehouse College, was our commencement speaker. There wasn't a vesper service or reception afterward or anything like that—just the ceremony. I wasn't excited about it. I had already lined up a job as a math teacher and wanted to get to it. Hurry up, start earning an income.

Our parents were so happy when A.D. and I graduated from college. Mom arrived for the graduation with her sister, Aunt Frieda. Dad was not able to come to the ceremony. Of course Aunt Callie was there. She rode the bus down from Dallas and had lunch with us before she headed back home. All of them were so proud.

Space race begins...

When I graduated from college in 1961, the space program was gearing up. The Russians had beaten the United States by putting the first man, Yuri Gagarin, into space for a 108-minute orbital flight. In May of 1961, Alan Shepard became the first American in space with a successful fifteen-minute suborbital flight.

Without question, the United States began to invest heavily in the space program. President Kennedy wanted to fast-track the space program and regain the lead. In his speech at Rice Stadium in Houston, Texas, on September 12, 1962, Kennedy laid out the charge, determined that the U.S. would be the leader in the space race, and announced a goal of putting an American on the moon before the end of the decade. President Kennedy directed a lot of money into science and mathematics to build the technological workforce needed to make this happen—and it did in July 1969.

Alan Shepard was the first American in space, but John Glenn became the first American to orbit the earth—orbiting three times on February 20, 1962. The country admired Glenn and wanted to know everything about him. He got a lot of attention because of his blond hair, blue eyes, and strong, outgoing personality. After his career as an astronaut, he became a U.S. senator, but later flew again in space.

The space program piqued my interest, and with Kennedy's support, there was a crack in the door for people of color. This was especially significant since our country was in the midst of the Civil Rights movement. I thought I might take a step into the industry and into space, thought that maybe there was a possibility...

The Baron Social Club – Prairie View A&M College, 1959.
(J.D. Oliver, third row, third from left; A.D. Oliver,
third row, second from left) (Author Collection)

J.D. Oliver – 1959 (Author Collection)

18

The twins in ROTC uniforms – 1958
J.D. (left), A.D. (right) (Author Collection)

J.D. and A.D. Oliver – Graduation Day 1961
(Author Collection)

Chapter 3

Family with Strength and Vision

Overview of Oliver family focusing on a special aunt
who graduated from college and supported J.D.
and A.D. so they could attend Prairie View.

My name is J.D. Oliver and my twin was A.D. Oliver. No names, just initials. The only difference is that I was named after our father, J.D. Sr.—I'm J.D. Jr. A.D. and I were born June 10, 1938 in Ledbetter, Texas. I was born thirty minutes earlier than A.D.

Our family roots and early education were in rural Ledbetter off Highway 290, but when A.D. and I entered the ninth grade, the family moved to Dime Box, Texas, about three or four miles across the county road from Ledbetter and 112 miles west of Houston. We went to Fairview High School in Dime Box.

A typical day, when A.D. and I were in school, was to get up in the morning about seven o'clock and have breakfast—the usual was bacon, syrup, oatmeal, milk, biscuits, and sausage. The whole family would eat together, then we would be off. We walked about a half mile to the Antioch School in Ledbetter when we were in elementary to the eighth grade. The teachers lived in the community and were within walking distance of the school as well. Myrtle Lacy was the principal.

After we moved to Dime Box and were in high school at Fairview, we would walk about two miles to school and get there about a quarter to nine. We would play basketball, if the weather was fair, until the bell rang at nine o'clock. We had math, then English, agriculture, and history—that was the whole day. Our studies at Fairview included geometry and algebra I and II. I really liked mathematics. It came easy for me. We had a small class and our teacher, Mr. Edwards, spent a lot of time explaining basic concepts.

George Washington Edwards taught mathematics and commuted from Gonzales. He rented a room in town during the week. Then he'd get in his car—a Chevrolet—and go home on the weekends, traveling about sixty or seventy miles. He taught algebra, trigonometry, geometry, and basic math. Mr. Edwards taught all the math grades, and he was the principal. We had four teachers for about one hundred students.

A.D. and I were good students, making As and Bs. I made As and a couple of Bs, and A.D. made straight As. We had recess before lunch, then an afternoon recess. A. D., Earl, and I did not eat lunch at school because it was too expensive. Ten cents a plate was a lot of money, so my sister Gladys ate. We had a good breakfast to hold us until we got home and ate supper.

It was fun being a twin during our high school years. We did try to fool the girls sometimes into thinking one was the other and vice versa. Oftentimes we dressed alike to confuse people even more. Some people could determine who was who because they had figured out a distinguishing mark or mannerism, or had made a distinction in our voices. Even our cousins had a difficult time telling us apart. As we grew older, one cousin claimed he could tell us apart when speaking to us on the telephone. I am not too sure about that.

All of us worked in the fields, picking cotton. A.D., our brother Earl, and I started picking cotton when we were in high school for money to purchase our school clothes and supplies. We would start as soon as school ended in May. We would chop first; then we would pick in July and August. It was hot. No one taught us how to pick cotton. We learned on our own. You figure out how not to prick your fingers and all that stuff. Put your fingers in the little boll and pull out the cotton. It would stick sometimes. Put your cotton in the sack and when you get your sack full, you carry your cotton to the scale and weigh it, then start over again. I remember that A.D. kept the numbers. We were paid thirty cents an hour and worked ten hours a day, so we made fifteen dollars a week chopping cotton. I don't know exactly how much I earned picking cotton, but I know what I earned chopping cotton.

Our uncle Kermit, who we nicknamed Uncle Spit, would write everything down. He was my mother's brother and drove a big truck to haul cotton pickers, carrying us to the field. He would write your score and at the end of the week, he would calculate the amount of time that you had picked. Add, multiply by some number, I don't remember. I could pick about four sacks in a day, two in the morning and two in the evening if the cotton was thick. A lot of cotton, a pretty thick sack, was about seventy pounds, depending on how long the sack was. Some people could pick ninety-five pounds. Uncle Spit would stay close to the scale, empty the cotton into the truck, and get the trailer filled. He carried the cotton to the gin, and the gin would separate out the seeds.

There would be bugs around like grasshoppers. We would see snakes, but they would run and weren't interested in us. Sometimes there would be bugs on the cotton. There were men, women, and children out there picking, sometimes whole families. Maybe twenty or twenty-five people in a large field, in our case I'd say forty to fifty acres, but sometimes larger than that.

We were quiet while picking, just trying to get the cotton as quickly as we could because that determined our money. When we were chopping or picking cotton, we had access to water. Someone would walk around with an open bucket and a cup and you dipped into the bucket to get your water. They would buy ice sometimes to keep the water cool. It wasn't too bad.

There is a difference between picking and chopping cotton. Picking cotton means taking the cotton out of the boll that is on the stalk. Chopping cotton means chopping the grass and weeds from around the stalk so it can grow stronger. I remember we lived about fifty miles from a place called Brazos Bottom, where we chopped cotton. We would commute from Dime Box to Brazos Bottom and work a ten-hour day, with only thirty minutes for lunch. I kept thinking while I was chopping cotton that I didn't want to do this for the rest of my life; it was just something I had to do to get through school. I was always glad when it was time to go back to school. I chopped cotton every summer until I graduated from high school. I did not go to the field that summer.

When A.D. and I graduated from Fairview, there were eight students in our class, and two of them were Olivers. There were four boys: William Cox, Sylvester Bullock, A.D., and me. The four girls were Marva Bethany, Delores Christmas, Mildred Lacey, and Lucy Benson.

The summer after high school graduation, and just before we went off to college, we got jobs working in Bryan, Texas, at a heating and air-conditioning company. That was so much better than working in the cotton fields. We wired houses and installed air conditioners. That was good money and we were able to buy clothes, shoes, and supplies. Every summer while we were in college at Prairie View, we would go back to Bryan on Highway 6 and get our jobs back.

After graduating from college, I returned to Bryan, but this time as a junior high math teacher and later as a high school math teacher.

Callie Oliver: "*We were her boys...*"

Callie Wilma Oliver was our aunt. She was quite a woman. A.D. and I were her favorites. In fact, she called us "her boys." She was a schoolteacher and graduated from Prairie View Normal and Industrial College with a bachelor's degree in English and Education on August 14, 1938. That was more than eighty years ago, almost unheard of for a woman in Texas at that time, but she was determined. Aunt Callie was one ambitious woman and pretty too—the first in our family to graduate from college. She did this at a time when a lot of Black people didn't have the opportunity go to college, or did not realize they could.

Aunt Callie first taught at Antioch Common School in Ledbetter and then moved to Dallas. A.D. and I would go up there to visit. We would ride the bus to stay with her in Dallas on weekends and for longer times during the summer. We spent our time talking about different things, but Callie would mostly talk about being at home, back in the country. She talked about other things, but she always emphasized education. She bought books for us and encouraged us to read. She would get really angry when it looked like we wouldn't follow her lead. We would tell her we were thinking about going into the Army, but she would say, "As long as there is a Black child, there will be a need for Black teachers." I think she figured the military was not for us, and that is one reason I didn't go into the Army. She thought the Army was not a good career and that soldiers were trained to kill people. That was something she did not approve of.

Callie just wanted us to go to college. She didn't push us into a certain subject, just whatever was needed to teach. She pressed us about going to Prairie View, though. She never said that she wouldn't support us if we didn't go to PV, but we felt that she wouldn't. She wanted us to figure out a way we could take care of ourselves and our families.

Aunt Callie was sort of strict. She wanted A.D. and me to do the same thing. She bought us clothes and dressed us alike. She made sure we ate healthy food—much like she did. Callie wasn't a big meat-eater, so she served us mostly vegetables and fruit. Sometimes we had chicken and ham—she made us a lot of ham sandwiches. We ate beets in the summertime, field peas—had to shell them—and fresh corn, just a regular healthy dinner. My dad grew a lot of vegetables and he would give them to her when she was back at Antioch, their home community. When she lived in Dallas, she would go to a store called Minyard and buy a lot of vegetables. She wanted us to have fresh food and not so much junk food. She was a healthy person, strict about eating, and stayed slim her entire life.

Callie was the youngest of my father's siblings and was part of his vision for family success. Back then, it was understood that a woman would just get married and have a husband who would take care of her, so she didn't need an education. My father had a different view for her success, and although he supported his sister, she earned money by working various jobs too.

Our aunt never married, never introduced a man to us. She wanted to get her education and take care of "her boys." Aunt Callie got it in her mind that she was going to send A.D. and me to college. We didn't have a say or a choice, either. She had decided we were going to go and that was it. She sat us down early in our junior year of high school and told us that she was going to pay for our schooling because our father had sent her to college, and she was going to do the same for us. Tuition was ninety dollars each semester and she was going to pay for A.D. and me. It was all set. Most people thought we were her actual children.

Aunt Callie had faith in God, encouraged education, and believed in land ownership. She was frugal, wasn't a fancy dresser or anything like that. She had a conservative appearance. Callie read newspapers—*Dallas Morning News*—plus *Ebony, Jet,* and *Ladies' Home Journal.* Back home in Ledbetter, she taught English at Antioch Common School and went to Antioch Baptist Church. She read the announcements at church and was a Sunday School teacher.

Callie was a smart and industrious woman. She purchased land by saving from her teaching salary and frugal living—one forty-four-acre tract, and then she inherited another tract with our father. She saved her money and started buying land. She bought a nice house—actually the best one in Ledbetter—and bought some nice pieces of furniture, which was a lot for a woman at that time. She went to the bank and negotiated that all on her own. I still have her little bank book. She bought her house at 10 percent interest from First National Bank, a white-owned bank, in Giddings, Texas. It's amazing that the bank even sold property to her because they probably wanted to know where her husband was or how she would repay the loan, but she didn't have any problems. They probably respected her because she was a teacher, a churchgoing woman, and they knew about her character.

When Callie moved to Dallas to teach at Arlington Park Elementary School, she was aggressive, buying a house and two lots close to Bishop College. She taught school during the week and went to church at Pleasant Grove Baptist Church on Sundays. She said she had a boyfriend at one time, but that relationship didn't last long. She never learned how to drive, never got a driver's license, and never had a car. She lived close to the school where she taught, less than a fourth of a mile, so she walked to and from school.

Our aunt gave all her property to A.D. and me—we leased the full tract to oil companies for drilling and split the proceeds. She had other nieces and nephews, but Callie had made up her mind that "her boys" were going to get the land. After she got older and couldn't handle the house in Ledbetter anymore, she sold it. The man who bought the house moved it off the property.

When A.D. and I began pursuing our technology careers and were hired at Lockheed Electronics in Houston, she was very proud. It's not that she wasn't proud of our teaching careers, but to know that we were a part of the space program was perhaps more than she could have imagined. She made sure to keep up with our progress by phone and letters. A.D. and I carried her to the Space Center for a tour several times, and she was impressed. Callie couldn't believe that the two of us were among the first African Americans at Lockheed Electronics. She didn't even think that was possible. We told her about our positions and duties, and she couldn't believe some of the things we were telling her. She was always present in our lives. Our aunt was there when I married Carolyne and when A.D. married Helen. She came to both weddings and rode from Dallas on the bus both times.

Callie fell and broke her leg in 1988. We had to put her in an assisted living facility. A.D. and I drove to Dallas to visit her quite often, and when we couldn't visit, we called her on the phone and talked to her at night. We stayed so close—she was like our other mother—and that continued until she died a few years after moving into the facility. I hated to see Callie pass away. If it wasn't for her, A.D. and I would not have been as successful as we were. It was difficult, but we just prayed about it and kept on going. We knew she had lived a full life and that was a comfort to us. Callie saw all the major events of our lives. Yeah, we were her boys, right up until the day she died on July 11, 1991.

Siblings and other family

Our brother, Earl, followed in our footsteps and went to Prairie View to study industrial education. A.D. helped him early on, but Earl paid for most of his education on his own. After graduation, he began his professional career teaching industrial education at Basile

High School in Basile, Louisiana. He was the first in our family to get a job outside of Texas, but he soon came back to wed his college sweetheart, Henrine Woods. They moved to Dallas, where their first son, Stephen Anthony Oliver, was born. Earl remained in education for a while, but decided to go into industry and was hired at Texas Instruments (TI)—a semiconductor, design, and manufacturing company. He later was hired at General Electric (G.E.) as a sales representative for electric turbines, and moved to New Jersey with his family. He continued to work for G.E., but went into business for himself—renting apartments and selling houses. While they lived in New Jersey, their second child, David, was born. Both of Earl's children grew up and were educated there. Earl lived in New Jersey for forty-two years. He passed away in 2016.

Our youngest sister, Mary Frances, was born when our parents were older. Unfortunately, she was born with a mental disability that made life a bit difficult for her. We all surrounded her with our love and support to help her feel she was no different. After graduating from high school, she had the desire to achieve and went to beauty school. She moved to Houston and lived with my family and me for a while. Our son, Jay, was a baby then, and Frances loved helping Carolyne care for him. She later married Charles Simon and had a son, Christopher. Frances, as we called her, was stricken with breast cancer and died in 1990.

I followed Aunt Callie's lead and sent my sister Gladys to college. I advised Gladys to go into education just as Callie had done for us, and she took my advice. Before she entered Prairie View, I took her shopping for clothes, bedding, and essentials she would need. If she wanted anything other than the basics for college, she would have to buy that herself. She got a job on campus in her third year as a matron in Evans Hall, one of the girls' dormitories. She got a loan that took care of her tuition, and I took care of the rest of her fees. She was able to finish in three and a half years by going to summer school.

She finished all the courses she needed to graduate in December 1968, but the graduation ceremony wasn't until May 1969.

Gladys was hired in January 1969 to teach third grade in Willis, Texas, and worked there for six years. Along with teaching those six years, she took summer and weekend classes at Prairie View and earned her master's degree in education. She later married Leslie Chandler II and moved to Giddings, Texas, where she was hired as a fourth-grade Language Arts teacher. She taught there for forty-one years. During that time, she had three children, all of whom attended Prairie View and earned Bachelor of Science (B.S.) degrees in agriculture.

Parents

Our mother and father were excited that their twin boys were in college. I imagine that my father went around doing a little bragging about us. Although he loved talking about his children, he and mom were married for a long time but never talked with us much about their personal lives. I wished that I had made the effort and had taken the time to learn more about them.

Dad was a quiet man, but he talked a lot with us about things that were happening in the world so we would be knowledgeable about things going on around us, but never much about himself. When A.D. and I were youngsters, a Black man was lynched in Waco, Texas. This happened before we went to Prairie View. Everybody knew about the incident. Our father talked about it at home, just discussed it in general. He didn't offer any advice or express any fear or concern; he just talked about it like you have a conversation about the news. It happened around the time that the *Brown versus Board of Education* decision was handed down in 1954. We found out that later, to enforce Brown, (President) Eisenhower sent the troops to Arkansas to protect the Little Rock Nine. Dad's reading the papers and listening to the radio kept us informed.

Our dad was one of seven children, with he and Callie being the youngest. He probably communicated with Callie more than with his other siblings, especially since they were so close. He preached a little bit and I remember his first sermon—"Who Shall I Send, and Who Will Go" (Isaiah 6:8). I also remember his prayer, "Almighty and merciful God. You are the creator and the Savior. You created us in love, and saved us in grace." His prayer has stayed with me, and I often include it in my prayers. He did some farming but wasn't successful. That's why we had to go out into the fields and pick cotton, because farming was not lucrative for him. He raised cattle and hogs, had chickens and turkeys. It was difficult to earn enough money with farming to care for the family because weather was such a huge factor, especially in the Lee County area where we lived. Sometimes he went out and worked odd jobs wherever he could. He even worked for a while in Galveston doing construction work just to support us. There was never any doubt that our father did everything he could to provide for his family.

As Dad's health continued to fail, we had to place him in a nursing home in Giddings. Gladys and her family lived near-by and could regularly check in on him. Dad was happy where he was, enjoyed the company of those around him, and had a room on the Highway 290 side of the facility. He wanted to look out of the window and, as he would say, "see people going to and from Houston". Dad passed on November 6, 1976 at age eighty-three.

Our mother was Corrie Lee Irving Oliver, and she and our father were both born in Lee County near Ledbetter, Texas. We called our mother "Mom", and she had a kind and quiet personality. She was one of ten in her family. We often wondered how she and Dad met and struck up conversation with both having quiet personalities. But they were comfortable with each other. For certain, Mom had a beautiful soprano voice and was often "on program" at funerals singing her favorite song, "The Lord Will Make a Way." She was a positive but firm person. When she spoke, that was it. We did not challenge her, and she, more than our father, was the disciplinarian.

Mom was valedictorian of her class, although the school only went to the tenth grade. She was excellent in English and spelling and could spell almost any word or term that you asked of her. She did not work outside the home; she stayed home and took care of the family. She was a real homemaker—did gardening, canning, quilting, and such. The nice part of all that is when we came home from school, she was there, and dinner was ready. Mom made sure we did all our chores before dark because we did not have electricity. We did our homework by kerosene lamps, and she made sure the glass lamp globes were clean so that we could see well. Our mother extended a warm welcome to anyone who would come to visit. Back then, visitors would just show up because no one had phones to call ahead. But Mom found a way to have a nice meal for everyone...always.

On December 17, 1969, our mother was out grocery shopping, preparing for her children to come home for Christmas. She became ill and passed away. Mom was fifty-five.

Life as a twin: A.D. and me

It has been quite a journey being an identical twin. During the eighty years of our lives together, our paths parted for only two years. I know that may be unusual even though we are twins, but it just happened. We stayed close and shared a lot of things. No one—not our parents, not Aunt Callie—tried to interest us in doing different things. Everyone was happy with us being together.

A.D. was the person who took the lead. He was the dominant personality and I was the quiet one, even though I was the firstborn. We called him the "boss." He was a top scholar, but I was right behind him. We did everything together, socially and academically. We dressed alike most of the time, and occasionally we would get into mischief being twins.

People had difficulty telling us apart, even in professional settings. I recall a time when we both applied for a teaching position at Southern University in Baton Rouge, Louisiana. A.D. was in the office handling his interview, and I was sitting out in the waiting area. A professor walked by and asked if I needed assistance. I said, "Well, I'm here for an interview." The professor said, "Oh, well, good luck," and went on down the hall.

A.D. came out, sat in the same chair, and I went in. The professor passed again and said, "Oh, you're still sitting here? I thought by now you would be in for the interview." A.D. said, "Well, no, I just sat down." The professor was perplexed and said, "But I saw you earlier." A.D. said, "No, I just got here." He wouldn't tell the professor anything different, and of course, the man walked away puzzled.

That's the big difference I see between A.D. and me. If you made a mistake and thought that I was A.D., I would immediately clarify and say, "Oh, no. I have a twin brother and you probably have me confused with him." But if you saw A.D. and thought it was me, A.D. would not always correct you; he would string you along just to see how you might respond. He would say something along the lines of "I have no clue what you're talking about. No, I haven't been there. No, I don't know." He wouldn't say that he had a twin brother and you may have seen the other one. He would not clarify but would let you walk off confused.

When we started working together at Lockheed Electronics at the Johnson Space Center, we tried not to dress alike. We lived together and, of course, rode together to work every day. Even after I got married and bought a home, A.D. persuaded the neighbors next door to sell their house to him so we could live next door to one another and continue to ride to work together. No matter how we tried not to dress alike, it would just happen. One day, he came out with exactly the same dress wear as mine. We were just the same. While working at Lockheed, we had secret clearances and wore badges, but people would have to look at the badges to tell us apart. They couldn't look in our faces and figure out who was who. Plus, both of us wore the same style of glasses. We both had the same haircuts and wore mustaches at the time. If there was something different about either one of us, I can't think of anything, even right down to politics—A.D. and I considered ourselves to be conservative Democrats.

We were well into adulthood before we started to part ways a bit and make our own paths. While we continued to live next door to one another, we began to do different things. We joined the same church in 1969—Wheeler Avenue Baptist Church—but for the first time, we were involved in different ministries. I was in the Courtesy Corps as an usher and on the church count team, counting the offering collected at services. A.D. was involved in the men's choir. He got the singing voice from our mom. I could sing, but I was a little bit shy about my voice.

We both started at Lockheed Electronics, but he left after seven years and went to work for McDonnell Douglas. I stayed with Lockheed until 1979, when I went to work for Singer-Link. A.D. taught, but never had a desire to teach long term as I did. He went into printing, becoming an entrepreneur, and I went to Prairie View to become a professor.

We stayed close to our other siblings with calls and visits. Both A.D. and I would call Earl, who lived with his family in New Jersey, and talk to him all the time. We also visited each other from time to time, visiting our sisters and their families often, and remained close with our nieces and nephews. We were a close-knit family.

After A.D. married Helen, the four of us were together a lot—going to church, church gatherings, dinners, and social events. I recall one fraternity gala when A.D. and Helen arrived before Carolyne and I did. One of the guests at the table did not realize I had a twin brother, so when A.D. arrived with Helen, they were shocked because they thought I had arrived with someone else. As they were discussing their concerns with one another, Carolyne and I arrived. That, of course, gave them great relief.

Carolyne and Helen would do a lot of shopping together—gone most of the day on Saturdays. They would come home with the car full of bags and packages, always working to make our homes comfortable. There were other couples we socialized with, some separate sets of friends, but most were church people. Our lives were spent close to each other in one way or another. We were not apart much and lived next door to one another forty-seven years.

36

The twins around 2 years of age (1940)
J.D. - left, A.D. – right (Author Collection)

J.D. and A.D., Fairview High Honor Students
– 1957 (Author Collection)

Dad – J.D. Oliver, Sr. (Author Collection)

Mom – Corrie Lee Oliver (Author Collection)

Callie Oliver – Graduation from Prairie View State
Normal School – 1938 (Author Collection)

The Prairie View State Normal
and
Industrial College of Texas

To all to whom these presents may come Greeting
Be it known that

Miss Callie Wilma Oliver

having completed the studies and satisfied the requirements for the
Degree of

Bachelor of Arts

has accordingly been admitted to that Degree with all the honors,
rights and privileges belonging thereto.

Given under the seal of the College at Prairie View, Texas,
on the 14th day of August A. D. nineteen hundred and thirty eight.

Callie Oliver's Degree - 1938

Chapter 4

Love, Marriage, Family, and Spiritual Life

*A look at the courtship and marriage to Carolyne,
adoption and childhood of Jay, early life as a family,
and the strengthening of their Christian faith.*

I got married first. Carolyne Bradley was the kind of person I was looking for—a good girl, a church girl—and she was exactly what I wanted. She grew up in Marlin, a small Texas town, was close to her family and well respected. She was a smart girl, and I learned she was quite a leader, into every activity and club possible in high school. Carolyne was in the band, played the clarinet, and was head majorette. She was in the choir and named Interscholastic League spelling champion for her school. That reminded me of my mom's spelling abilities. She was in girls' clubs, worked in her home church, was the announcement clerk, ushered, in the church choir, led Sunday School classes, and so much more. She was a contestant for Miss Texas High in 1963. The organizers had the pageant on Prairie View's campus, but I had graduated two years earlier and didn't know her then.

Carolyne was valedictorian of her high school class and came to Houston in 1964 to attend the University of Houston (UH), one year after the university integrated. She was in the first integrated class of students who graduated four years later in 1968. Carolyne went to work for Houston Lighting and Power (now Reliant Energy) and was the first female and the first African American hired in the market research division. She was busy making her mark.

We met at Wheeler Avenue Baptist Church in October 1969. There were a lot of young singles at the church—many were either UH or Texas Southern University (TSU) graduates. Carolyne and some of her UH friends joined Wheeler while in college and continued to worship there. It was not unusual for the singles to congregate and visit after church, and that is where I first met her. I'll never forget. We were standing around talking about the TSU-Southern University football game when we first struck up a conversation.

As usual, A.D. was doing all the talking and I was quietly observing. What caught my attention was Carolyne's bright smile as she engaged in conversation with us. In December of the same year, Carolyne was planning a Christmas party and invited A.D. and me. Unfortunately, we could not attend because our mother had passed away just a couple of weeks before and, as I told her, we had promised our sisters and Dad that we would return home for the Christmas holidays. After I returned to Houston, I felt I needed to make up for not attending her party, so I called to check on how the party went. During the conversation, I asked her out for our first date in January 1970. We went to a movie at a nearby theater and then to dinner. After a few dates, I knew she was the one, and in February, 1970, I asked her to marry me.

After deciding to get married in September, we spent the spring and summer planning our wedding and spent almost every evening after work together. We practically did everything together. I would call her during the day, sometimes twice a day, and we would plan our evening—go to Hermann Park after work to relax, feed the ducks—especially in the summer—or go to dinner. I even began to pick her up on Sundays to go to church and dinner. One of our favorite places to eat was the Groovey Grill owned by Faurice and Jessie Prince. On Sundays, the Grill served cornish hens and dressing and quickly became a favorite place to eat. Many of the singles were pairing off, and we had a good idea who was going to marry whom. Most of us would meet at the Grill after church.

We were married on Saturday, September 5, 1970 at the University of Houston chapel by our pastor, Rev. William A. Lawson, and had our reception in the ballroom of the UH Student Center. Our wedding was a major event for our families. Carolyne's family and many friends from Marlin attended, and my family and friends were there, including Aunt Callie, who rode down on the bus from Dallas. I saw my family in formal attire for the first time, and could see the joy on their faces to participate in our wedding.

A.D. married about two years later in 1972. His wife, Helen, is from Bryan, and we knew her older brothers when we worked in Bryan during the summer months while we were in college. Years later, after Helen graduated from college, A.D. and Helen began dating and were married in December 1972. Their wedding was in Bryan, and once again, our aunt Callie rode the bus from Dallas.

There must be some truth in the saying, "opposites attract." Carolyne and I really complemented each other. I was probably more comfortable in our relationship because, much like my twin, Carolyne was the talker and I was the quiet one. It was probably easier for me to adjust to our marriage than it was for her, as an only child. It took her a while to understand the relationship between A.D. and me. She would say: "I don't understand what it is like being a twin. I am an only child, so not only do I not understand being a twin, I don't understand sibling relationships. Why do you always listen to what your brother is saying? Why do you always have to go over to his house? Why can't you figure things out for yourself and not have to get your brother's input? I don't understand this." I guess she had some difficulty understanding that A.D. and I had made decisions and done things together all our lives. Living next door to one another was just another example of how inseparable we were.

I also had to understand and respect her drive and need to get things done. She took the lead in making our home comfortable, making friends, planning our social calendar, entertaining in our home, and most of all, ensuring we always remained involved in our church. Just as A.D. was the one to see to it that we always had a church home, Carolyne was the one to get up and get us going to church on Sunday mornings.

Take driving, for instance. I really didn't like those short trips around town at all, didn't like stopping at all those traffic lights. If we took a trip, Carolyne would drive through the small towns until we got on the open highway and then I would take the wheel. She always enjoyed driving. Now that I don't drive at all, she is still the one to get us wherever we need or want to go. Driving just seems a natural for her.

People often ask us what the secret is for being married fifty years. Carolyne and I both agree that you must first be rooted in your faith; then you must love, respect, and appreciate one another—appreciate and accept the differences. Be willing to go through the good times and the bad, knowing you can lean on and depend on each other. Remain true to the marriage vows, "for richer or poorer, for better for worse, in sickness and in health." Be committed to working hard to make your dreams come true—we sure did.

Family

When we first got married, like most young couples, we definitely wanted to have children, but we were unable to conceive. Neither A.D. nor I could have biological children. There was probably a medical reason why we did not have children. It may seem unusual, but I guess our DNA was about the same.

Carolyne and I discussed our options, and she suggested that we adopt. She had the thought at one time that she wanted to be a foster mother and just have a bunch of children to love and care for. She also considered adopting a child with special needs because she had it in her heart to give. We talked more about adoption, but at the time it was just conversation.

Carolyne was working at Houston Lighting and Power (HL&P) in the market research division, and recalls that there were few African Americans in professional positions at the time. Although she was the only African American and the only woman working with all white men in her department, she did not encounter any overt racial or gender problems. Many of her coworkers were recent college graduates, newly married, and they seemed to keep up with one another. Carolyne often talked about some of the senior staffers who seemed to work well with the recent hires. They would have lunch together, and we went to one another's homes for dinner. I was having a similar experience in my workplace at Lockheed—it was a sign of the times, as corporate was adjusting to a diversified workforce.

Late spring of 1976, the transmission and distribution division at HL&P went on strike. It was an unusual time in our lives. Carolyne and I had heard of, but had never participated in a strike. Those in certain divisions in the downtown offices were transferred to the power plants. Carolyne was transferred to the H.O. Clarke plant, which was near our home. That was a true blessing for us and gave me a sense of relief because some people had to drive across town to their assignments. They were working twelve-hour shifts—twelve hours on, twelve hours off. The shifts ran either from 11 to 11 or 1 to 1. As Carolyne shared with me, the main objective for those who were brought out from the office was to keep the power plants operational, generating electricity twenty-four hours a day, seven days a week. The supervisors at the plants were not on strike and were there to guide those who came from the downtown offices. That was a huge learning curve. The smaller power plants came online as the demand for more electricity rose—during the summer months, peak hours in the heat of the day—and then the plants were brought offline. At the H.O. Clarke plant, they were up and down every day. They would come online at the peak need during the day and come offline in the evening. Bringing a power plant up and down was truly a new and different experience for her. But then, Carolyne will do what she has to!

The HL&P staff in the sales and market research divisions were being paid extra for the longer shifts, so with the increase in income, Carolyne and I had a more serious discussion about adoption. We had decided she would stay home the first few months with our child and not have to work, so we set aside this extra money and decided to go through the process of adoption. One morning before I left for work—guess she must have been on the 11-to-11 shift—I agreed that she should go ahead and call the adoption agency.

So, in the summer of 1976, Carolyne called DePelchin Faith Home—a respected adoption agency with a good track record of placing babies with families. By the fall, she and I prepared to bring our child home. It was like clockwork. We believed that there would be a long waiting period and it might be months or years before an adoption would take place, but it was a fast turnaround.

Our caseworker was Mrs. Reynolds, and she did a series of visits to our home, the same home we live in now. She wanted to see the room that would be the baby's room. We had a spare bedroom with large windows and a built-in changing table that could later be converted to a child's desk that was perfect for the nursery/child's room. So in late September, the agency called to let us know we had passed all the requirements and they had a baby boy ready to be placed with us. Our son was born in August but was a premature baby and the agency wanted to be sure he was healthy before placing him.

Knowing that we were going to be blessed with a baby, it was time for us to select a name. We wanted our son to have part of Carolyne's name and part of my name. Her maiden name is Bradley and she really liked the name Brad, and my initials are J.D., but she was determined we had to spell out J-A-Y. We could not decide if we wanted to name our son Bradley Jay or Jay Bradley. After much thought and discussion, we named him Jay Bradley because we thought J.B. Oliver had a special ring to it! We called him Brad as he was growing up. However, when he went to first grade, his teacher called him by his first name, Jay. From that point on, he became Jay. Our son tells us he is happy that he was named Jay because he didn't like the name Brad.

So, in October, Carolyne told the HL&P staff that she was going to take a leave of absence because we were adopting our baby. They gave her a big baby shower on her last day. While Carolyne and I were getting the paperwork in order for the adoption, our soon-to-be son was being cared for in a foster home. We drove over to DePelchin to pick up our son. As we walked into Mrs. Reynolds' office, we noticed her wall was covered with pictures of babies she had placed. Carolyne oohed and aahed over the baby boys because she knew we were getting a boy. A worker walked in and Mrs. Reynolds said, "Mr. and Mrs. Oliver, here is your baby!"

"Oh, look at him! He is adorable!" Carolyne took him into her arms and was squealing with excitement. He never cried, was never fidgety or upset. He was a quiet baby. Carolyne held him, and then I held him. We felt blessed to have our son!

We wrapped Jay in the same blanket that Carolyne's mother wrapped her in when she was a baby. The foster mother sent along Jay's pacifier and items he was familiar with—including the name of his pediatrician, details about his feeding schedule, and other important information. We kept the same pediatrician for him until he was eighteen. We still have his pacifier and the blanket we wrapped him in the day we brought him home. Carolyne hopes we can wrap our grandchildren in it someday. It would be nice to get three generations out of that blanket if we could.

After settling in at home the first night, and looking at the feeding schedule, Carolyne figured she would have to get up at 4 a.m. to feed Jay. She urged me to keep our bedroom door open so that she could hear him if he cried. The next morning, Carolyne woke up in a panic. "Oh! The baby! Did he cry! I didn't hear him!" She raced over to his room, looked in the crib, and Jay was sleeping peacefully. The first night at home and he slept straight through. It was as if he knew, "This is home, and I can relax." He responded to us as though he knew we were his parents.

I went off to work and Carolyne said she spent the entire first full day cuddling and holding Jay. She worked on bonding by taking him out of the crib every morning and laying him on her chest and stomach as he drifted back to sleep, creating a mother-son bond that is true today. As Jay grew up, he became Carolyne's "running buddy." Jay claims that he learned how to drive from Carolyne because they went everywhere together.

Our caseworker told us that it was very important to tell Jay as early as possible that he was adopted. Carolyne knew of a family who had adopted and the drama it caused once the child found out about the adoption from others rather than the parents. No one in that family talked about it. Adoption was hush-hush back then. We were determined that Jay would not go through the same trauma of finding out about his adoption later in life.

So, one day as they were riding home from Texas Southern University Child Development Lab, where Jay was in preschool, Carolyne was trying to figure out how to tell Jay about his adoption. Carolyne knew that he was a big comic book fan and loved the DC Comics heroes. She brought up Superman, one of Jay's favorite characters, and told him how his family on Krypton knew the planet was going to explode, so they put him on a spaceship to send him to Earth so he could be saved. Jay knew the story and Carolyne said, "Well, you're like Superman!" She outlined the fictional parallel and how it applied to his life as someone whose biological parents loved him enough to let him go and be adopted by people who weren't his biological parents but who would love him. She told him that he was a special baby because he had two sets of parents.

"He loved that," Carolyne said. He told his friends down the street, "I'm special. You only have one set of parents, I have two. I am like Superman."

There was an incident with a neighborhood boy who told Jay that his mother remembers Carolyne being pregnant. Jay came running home demanding that she tells his friend that he was adopted. The two boys were arguing about whether Carolyne had been pregnant. Jay had accepted his adoption.

Jay tells Carolyne and me that he is glad we adopted him. He sometimes thinks about where he would be at this point in his life if we hadn't. He says that he is grateful for being brought up in a loving family. Jay seems to us to be a special person in many ways. He is a caring and compassionate person and seems to have an innate ability to understand the needs of others. We are proud of the person he has become.

We discussed adopting another child—a girl—to have a classic American family. We thought a second adoption would be good when Jay reached two or three years of age. However, we never followed through. Carolyne had begun thinking of going back to work, and believed it would have been difficult not being able to stay home with the second child and give her the same time and attention we gave Jay. I started working at Prairie View and began building a computer science program when Jay was about six, and I was only home on the weekends. Carolyne said she didn't want to try to raise two children with my being away from home during the week and not being able to give both children the time and attention they deserved.

Jay has begun looking for his biological family to satisfy his curiosity and know his roots. Carolyne helped him with the search and Jay has found a couple of cousins. They keep in touch and Jay has learned that his biological family is a large one. But as he tells us, "You are my parents, and that is all that matters!"

Spiritual Life

When we were children, A.D. and I attended Antioch Baptist Church in Ledbetter. It was our parents' church and, as far back as I can remember, we went there. As with most rural communities, Antioch was the community church, organized in 1877 with Rev. L.S. Stillwell as its first pastor. The first church building was built in 1879. Shortly thereafter, the Antioch Common School was built, which was where everyone in the community went. The original Antioch church building no longer exists, but the Antioch Common School has been renovated many times over and today is the Antioch Baptist Church.

When we were growing up, we went to church one Sunday out of a month—the fourth Sunday. We had Sunday school first thing in the morning at 9 or 9:30 and church would start about eleven o'clock. BTU (Baptist Training Union) was on Sunday evenings after supper. It was a small church and Rev. Lucius Henegan was the pastor.

We didn't take communion like we do today. Communion was only served during baptism. Baptism Sunday was also Communion Sunday. Baptism was first, communion was served, then we would

LOVE, MARRIAGE, FAMILY, AND SPIRITUAL LIFE   53

have service, so we might have been in church all day. I can remember when I joined church. It was the morning service. We were having revival with our pastor, and our parents encouraged us. A.D. and I were okay with going up to give our lives to the Lord. You joined and you were baptized. You confessed your faith and had to sit on the "mourners' bench." We sat on the bench with Lawrence Williams, a neighbor's child.

We had to wait until the next service to get baptized, the next fourth Sunday. I remember it well. We had Sunday School that morning and then regular service. We had to put on our work clothes, and the deacons carried us down to the pond. They had service by the water, a program, and most of the church was there. They baptized A.D. and me together, put us under and brought us back up, then Lawrence was baptized. They dried us off, we celebrated with communion, then church service, and that was that.

A.D. kept us more devout as we grew up and became adults. Sometimes, I might not have wanted to go to church, but that's one thing he insisted on, making sure we went. I could have easily slept in a little bit. When he was teaching in Texarkana and I was teaching in Bryan, I didn't go to church too often. I went to Shiloh Baptist Church in Bryan a few times, but not often, because A.D. wasn't around to encourage me. One thing I can say about A.D. is that he was the most involved of the two of us. He was more active when he was a child and into different things. When we went to Fisk University in Nashville, Tennessee, East Texas State, and Southern University in Baton Rouge, A. D. found a church. He made sure we were under Watch Care. When we were at Wiley College in Marshall, Texas, we went to a Methodist church. He did the same thing when we came to Houston. He would be first to ask, "When are we going to church?" He was the one who found Wheeler Avenue and we went together. He wanted to find a church home close to where we lived.

My favorite Scripture is Psalm 23—

The Lord is my shepherd; I shall not want. He maketh me to lie down in green pastures: he leadeth me beside the still waters. He restoreth my soul: he leadeth me in the paths of righteousness for his name's sake. Yea, though I walk through the valley of the shadow of death, I will fear no evil: for thou art with me; thy rod and thy staff they comfort me. Thou preparest a table before me in the presence of mine enemies: thou anointeth my head with oil; my cup runneth over. Surely goodness and mercy shall follow me all the days of my life: and I will dwell in the house of the LORD for ever.

I recite that scripture regularly today as I have found it to be comforting. When I reflect on the journey my life has taken, I know that the Lord is and has always been my shepherd. I don't know where I would be without Him.

In terms of my professional life, I didn't share my love of God with anyone while on the job, but now I would. I just didn't do it, and A.D. didn't either. Early on, we kept our spiritual lives and our daily lives separate—don't really know why—although at times we would invite others to visit our church. Some joined our church after visiting, even becoming church leaders.

Wheeler Avenue Baptist Church is our family church in Houston. Rev. William A. Lawson is the founding pastor. Carolyne joined in 1966 while a student at UH. I joined in 1969, and our son, Jay, was christened as a baby in 1976 and baptized by Rev. Lawson in 1982. We are all active there. Carolyne sang in the college choir, read the announcements, and welcomed the visitors, was a member and president of the Southwest Circle, is now on the Courtesy Corps (usher corps), and leads one of the ministries. Just as she was active in church growing up, she is still active now.

Jay grew up in the church and was active in Boy Scouts, becoming an Eagle Scout during his senior year in high school. When he went to college at Hampton University in Virginia, some of the students there were Wheeler members as well. It seems no matter where you go, you will run into Wheeler members or former members.

Now I tell people to come to Wheeler, not just because of the dynamic preaching, but because my faith has grown. I remember when Rev. Cosby became our associate pastor, some twenty-two years ago. He was a young graduate from seminary and was highly recommended by Rev. Dr. Jeremiah Wright, a longtime friend to Rev. Lawson. Rev. Wright and Rev. Cosby are both from Chicago. Once Rev. Cosby became associate pastor, Rev. Lawson gave him the task of building a Sunday evening service called "Sunday Night Live" to appeal to college students and young adults. Our church is located between two major universities—the University of Houston and Texas Southern, making it ideal for attracting singles and young adults. Rev. Cosby was remarkably successful in growing that service. He's a great preacher, a good singer, and on occasion directs the choir. He is a graduate of Fisk University and was the student choir director there. He knows good music and wants to hear good music. Good singing and good preaching make for an unforgettable worship experience!

Rev. Lawson, renowned pastor, visionary leader, devout teacher, and civil rights leader decided to retire and was looking for a replacement. Pastor Lawson said he was looking for someone who could take his place and grow the church—take it to the next level. Several preachers came in to preach sermons during the selection process. We were comfortable and familiar with Rev. Cosby's preaching because he was already the associate pastor. But the congregation was still given the opportunity to vote. Rev. Dr. Marcus D. Cosby was voted in and installed in 2004. Rev. Lawson still preached during the transition, but once Rev. Cosby became senior pastor, Rev.

Lawson stepped down and was named pastor emeritus. He still attends Sunday services when possible, which is almost every Sunday; and still preaches or prays on occasion, when his health allows. Rev. Lawson had a great vision for Wheeler Avenue, and it has come to fruition.

Pastor Cosby has been going strong since he took the reins—doing exactly what Pastor Lawson had hoped—growing the church, increasing the number of ministries and services to the congregation and community, and building a more intergenerational church with activities for every age group. Sometimes we have as many as forty people join church at one service. During the more than sixteen years that Pastor Cosby has been senior pastor, our membership has grown from the twenty-one charter members in 1962 to over 19,000—God has blessed Wheeler Avenue!

During the Thanksgiving holidays, Carolyne and I go to service at the neighborhood church, Brentwood Baptist. For years, Wheeler Avenue and Brentwood have had a joint pre-Thanksgiving service, and I thoroughly enjoy worshipping with the two congregations. Rev. Dr. Joe Samuel Ratliff, pastor of Brentwood Baptist Church, was at Wheeler before being called to Brentwood. Rev. Ratliff was A.D.'s pastor when he moved his membership to Brentwood. We feel like family at both churches.

Wheeler is building a new sanctuary to accommodate the growing membership. Currently we hold four services each Sunday, and Pastor Cosby preaches all of them. Sometimes we will have a visiting preacher or one of the staff ministers will preach, but for the most part, Pastor Cosby takes the pulpit. That is just how committed he is to the Lord's calling. Can't wait to move into the new church!

Carolyne and J.D.'s Wedding Day - September 5, 1970
University of Houston Chapel (Author Collection)

Dad at Wedding (Author Collection)

Ruby Weathers (Carolyne's Mother)
at Wedding (Author Collection)

Carolyne and J.D. picking up Baby Jay
at DePelchin Home - 1976 (Author Collection)

Father/son hug at Christmas (J.D. and Jay)
December 25, 2007 (Author Collection)

Antioch Baptist Church (Organized in 1877 and still in existence.) Home Church for J.D. (Author Collection)

Chapter 5

Early Teaching Days

J.D. and A.D. at Wiley College,
Southern University—1965 through 1968;
teaching at HBCUs in the 1960s; education at Fisk.

In my senior year at Prairie View, the first thing I wanted to do was get a deferment from the Army, and the second thing was to graduate and go teach somewhere. Teaching math or science could get you an automatic deferment, and our aunt Callie wanted us to teach anyway, so both A.D. and I chose that path.

Dad checked on deferments with the Draft Office in Giddings. Every little town had an office to handle signing up young men for the military. A lady from the Draft Office called our father and told him that many boys from the area were going into the military. He wanted us to get an education, so A.D. and I went to see the lady, sat down with her, and completed the paperwork to prove that we were students. We were eligible and got our deferment without any difficulty.

During that time, there were few options for African American male college graduates outside of the military. You could either go into industry or go into teaching. Companies hired few African Americans in professional positions when I was set to graduate, so for me, it was teaching.

After graduation in 1961, I applied to teach at E.A. Kemp High School, but was recruited to start teaching at Neal Junior High. Later I went to Kemp High, both in the Bryan Public School System. The principal at Neal was Dr. C.D. Yancy and he needed a math teacher. Roy Pace, who also graduated from PV, was already teaching math and told me about Dr. Yancy, whom I knew from my days of working in Bryan in the summer. So, Dr. Yancy reached out and gave me the job. The pay was $3,400 a year—nine months actually, and increased to $4,000 the next year. That was a nice salary at that time, but I taught for only two years in the public school system—one year at Neal Junior High and one year at Kemp High School. Everything was still segregated, so I only taught Black students.

I was familiar with the Bryan area since I had worked there during the summers when I was in college. During those days there was not much housing available for young teachers, so most of us rented rooms from people who owned homes, creating extensions of our own families. With the help of Dr. Yancy and one of my PV classmates, George Vault, who lived in Bryan, I was able to find housing with a lady named Willie Neal. She taught elementary school and was respected in the community. She became like a mother to me and I felt very much at home.

Once I settled in with my job and a place to live, one of the first things I did was to buy a car—my very first. I was so excited...no more riding on the bus, train, or jacking up that thumb to catch a ride along the road to get me where I was going! I bought a brand-new 1962 white Chevrolet from Corbusier Chevrolet Company on College Avenue in Bryan. I will never forget that first purchase.

The Chevy was a good car. It carried my brother and me across the country to a lot of places as we pursued our education and teaching careers. I gave that car to my sister Gladys when she graduated from college, and then I purchased a black and white Toyota Corona. After Gladys got her first teaching job, she was able to buy her own new car.

When I went to Bryan to teach, A.D. went back to Fairview High School in Dime Box and served as principal and head teacher for one year. He was the unofficial supervisor of teachers. Near the end of his first year at Fairview, he got a call from Dunbar High in Texarkana, Texas, because they needed someone to start an electronics program in high school. He accepted the job and was in Texarkana for one year. Those two years were the first and only time in our lives we were apart.

I was okay with teaching at Kemp, but I kept thinking about working in industry. I knew I could do it, but African Americans were not being readily hired, so it was just a thought. There weren't many options, but I thought that by going back to school, I could better prepare myself for teaching and perhaps, one day, the space program.

I did not like teaching in high school because of the discipline problems. You went in prepared to teach, but you had to spend most of your time disciplining students, making them sit down and be quiet. After two years of working in public schools, I decided I wanted more and applied for a National Science Foundation (NSF) grant to participate in the Fisk University Academic Year Institute for junior high and high school mathematics and science teachers. A.D. also liked the idea of furthering his education, so he applied, and we were both accepted into the NSF program at Fisk in Nashville, Tennessee. This meant my brother and I would be traveling out of the state of Texas for the first time, but this was an opportunity for me to expand my math and science skills and perhaps prepare for teaching at the college level, because I was done with high school teaching. The grant was about $3,400—close in range to my teaching salary, paving the way for me to make the transition. Although I did not like teaching high school kids, I still applied for a leave of absence for job security. My request was denied because public school systems did not grant leaves and that meant after the Fisk program ended, I would be looking for a job.

Our family was excited about A.D. and me being accepted for the NSF grant. Dad, who generally had little to say about the educational decisions we made, was very happy. He carried the information about our acceptance into the program up to the Giddings newspaper so they could run an article. This really made the family proud, especially Aunt Callie.

A.D. and I drove up to Nashville together in my Chevrolet. This worked well for me because A.D. could do most of the driving and share expenses as we advanced our education. Our country was in the midst of the Civil Rights Movement at that time, and A.D. and I were traveling in an unfamiliar part of the Deep South. The NAACP field secretary, Medgar Evers, had been assassinated in Jackson, Mississippi. Governor George Wallace had stood in the doors of the University of Alabama to stop Black students from attending. Dr. Martin Luther King had led the March on Washington in August of that year. This was a particularly challenging time for our country. Although we were miles away from these incidents, we were in the part of the country riddled with civil unrest.

There we were. Our car quit working on the highway just outside of Nashville. We knew we had to get out and walk to find a service station. We had read and heard about the racial unrest, but we did what we had to do. We found a service station run by a white man not too far up the road. We told him our problem and he gave us a ride back to our car, fixed it, and we were on our way—not a hint of trouble. A.D. admitted that incident made a true believer out of him that God was watching over us, and he realized then that "the Lord will make a way."

The Fisk program was eight months long—September 1963 to May 1964. The focus of our studies was mathematics, physics, and chemistry, and included a six-week period spent at the Oak Ridge Institute of Nuclear Studies as a member of the Oak Ridge Science Lecture Demonstration Program. This was a great opportunity because it allowed me to study at one of the nation's largest science and research facilities (birthplace of the atomic bomb), and prepared me to be a better math and science teacher.

While at Fisk, we lived in a place called the Richardson House, located on the campus. Other program participants lived there with us, and we all ate in the cafeteria with the students. The food was fair, but there was a fish place down the street from Richardson. We loved that fish and ate there a lot.

John F. Kennedy was assassinated while we were in Tennessee. I was studying when one of the members of our group came in and said that President Kennedy had been killed in Dallas. We learned that Governor John Connally was shot and wounded but survived. Everyone was sad because we knew Kennedy was committed to civil rights and was a strong advocate for math and science because of his push for the space program. I remember seeing the news showing Lyndon Johnson taking the oath of office on Air Force One with Kennedy's wife Jackie standing beside him. She still had on the bloodstained suit—a terrible time for our nation.

America was in such turmoil during the early Civil Rights Movement led by Dr. King. President Kennedy was working to pass legislation favorable for Black people. After his assassination, it was President Johnson who really pushed the Movement forward by signing the 1964 Civil Rights Bill. I had more positive feelings about Johnson because he was from Texas, a Southerner who became a senator, the vice president, and ultimately president of the United

States. That was a major accomplishment at the time. Johnson became vice president because Kennedy wanted to carry some portion of the South in the 1960 election, so he selected Johnson as his running mate. Johnson knew how to talk to Southern people and tell them what they needed and wanted to hear. I remember some of the old senators he worked with, such as Sam Rayburn, who was Speaker of the House. I believe Johnson made more progress with civil rights than Kennedy would have because he was from the South and "knew how to reach across the aisle." If Kennedy had lived, he might not have been able to push civil rights legislation through like Johnson did.

Wiley College

I finished my work at Fisk and Oak Ridge, so I came home in late May 1964. I had already decided that I wanted to teach at the college level instead of high school, so I applied to several colleges. Wiley College in Marshall, Texas, came through. They needed a math and science teacher and offered me a position, so I drove up to Marshall. I met the vice president, who asked me if I was ready to teach, and I said yes!

Again, A.D. rode along to keep me company. When we got there, the vice president said they needed another math teacher. A.D. was great in math, so he landed a job too. There we were together again, teaching. We taught at Wiley for one year.

Classes were small at Wiley, with men and women in the same classroom. I had about five students in physical science and also taught basic science and math. There was another professor, Mr. Williams, who taught advanced math.

A.D. and I lived in a big house on Highway 80. Dr. Thomas W. Cole, Sr., the university president, contacted the lady who owned the home and arranged for us to have a place to stay. We had the house to ourselves for one year and the rent was cheap. We had five rooms, including a stove and refrigerator. A.D. was the cook and I was the dishwasher, but we ate out a lot. There was a boardinghouse not too far from the campus and we ate lunch there, pay as you go. We were living large…oh, yes.

My studies at Oak Ridge and teaching at Wiley were rewarding and made me want to do more in the field of education. Aunt Callie's words continued to ring in my head— "As long as there are Black children, there will be a need for Black teachers." Teaching at Wiley reinforced my desire to teach at the college level and to learn as much as I could in the math and science fields. Things were changing rapidly with the focus on the space program, and more people were needed in the math and science arena. There was a critical shortage of African Americans in math and science, so much so that colleges and universities, especially Black colleges, were scouting all over for teachers. While at Wiley, my brother and I were recruited by Southern University in Baton Rouge, Louisiana, to teach math. So, off we went to expand our experiences.

We liked to go home during the summer, whenever possible, to check on our parents and give them updates on what we were doing. The summer between our time at Wiley and going to Southern wasn't any different, but what was distinctively different this time was our trip to Southern. It was just before the beginning of the fall semester and our time to report to work when we took off to Louisiana, only to arrive during Hurricane Betsy. Of course A.D. and I had not experienced a hurricane, so for us, it was just a terrible rainstorm. We didn't know the dangers of a hurricane, so we drove right on into Baton Rouge. We stayed temporarily with a family in Scotlandville as recommended by Vice President E.C. Harrison until our permanent living facilities were ready. It was only in the conversation with the family that we realized the storm was a hurricane. Once again, the Lord protected us as we were spared through the storm. After the storm was over, we found the place where we were to stay during our time at Southern and began to enjoy and experience Louisiana cuisine, especially gumbo and crawfish.

I was at Southern for two years and met many wonderful people in the math department. One such person was Dr. Delores Spikes, who later became president of the university, and the other person was Carolyn Jacob, one of the math professors, who was a mentor to A.D. and me. Although I enjoyed and appreciated the teaching opportunity at Southern, I continued to pursue opportunities to study math and science when and wherever possible. My brother and I sought graduate programs and summer institutes at Ball State University in Indiana, the National Institute of Health in Bethesda, Maryland, the University of California at Berkeley, and the University of Oklahoma. The National Science Foundation (NSF) was sponsoring numerous summer institutes and workshops on different college campuses, and I wanted to be a part of it. A.D. and I applied and were accepted to the NSF Summer Institute on Development in Modern Physics at Vanderbilt University in Nashville during the summer of 1966.

I felt at home in that part of the country because I had spent eight months at Oak Ridge. I spent a lot of time in the library and laboratories at Vanderbilt during the summer, which was okay because the weather was hot. Better to be indoors studying instead of in the heat, which reminded me of when I was young and working the cotton fields. Again, I met professors who encouraged me to consider pursuing a graduate degree. I gave it some thought at the time, but took no action. At the end of the institute, I returned home and attended a conference in the last few weeks of summer at Trinity University in San Antonio just before going back to work at Southern.

In the summer of 1967, we were off again. This time, we were attending the NSF Summer Institute for College Teachers of Mathematics to study Modern Mathematics at the University of Wisconsin (UW) in Madison. Never any time to waste as we continued to expand our knowledge in math and science.

Our trip to Wisconsin was by train. This was exciting for us because we had never ridden a train nor traveled that far north. I left my car at home, and a neighbor, whom we called "Jet" Benson, took us to Hearne, Texas, to catch the train. We arrived in Madison in the middle of the summer and were surprised at how cool the weather was. Most of the institutes we had attended were in the South where the weather was warm. This was definitely a change for us. We did not have our car and were unable to drive around and explore the surrounding areas. So, most of our time was spent in the library, classrooms, and around the campus of UW. In many ways, this was a different and rewarding experience.

When the institute ended, we returned home as usual to share our experience with our family. After a few days, we were off again to Southern University to begin our second year of teaching. As the 1967–68 academic year at Southern ended, I learned that the University of Oklahoma grant did not come through, which meant we had to seek other summer study opportunities. We found ourselves at East Texas State University at Commerce in the summer of 1968. We were enrolled as special students taking courses in math and computer science—including COBOL, FORTRAN, and Assembly Languages. We felt studies in math and computer science would open new opportunities for us. It was then we decided not to go back to teach at Southern, but rather seek scholarship opportunities to pursue graduate degrees in math and computer science.

During that summer, a representative from Lockheed Electronics was recruiting on campus. A couple of students came to the area where A.D. and I were working in the lab and told us that a recruiter was there. We went to see him because we wanted to consider all opportunities. He was looking for people in science and engineering to work at Lockheed in Houston at the Space Center. The recruiter talked to A.D. and me at the same time, but didn't say that he was recruiting African Americans. We just felt he was without actually saying it. We were invited to prepare an application, and we did.

By the end of the summer, the program at East Texas State ended. We had not yet begun our search for graduate programs in math and computer science, and had not yet heard anything about the Lockheed position. So, we applied and were accepted at Texas A&M University in College Station to work in the data center. A&M had a graduate program I could apply to later, and being in their data center gave me an opportunity to apply the lessons I had learned at East Texas State. Just as we were getting settled in at Texas A&M, we learned that we had been accepted for employment at Lockheed at the NASA Johnson Space Center in Houston. I saw this as an open door, tendered my resignation to Texas A&M in January 1969 and was off to begin a career in corporate America. Finally, my dream was coming true!

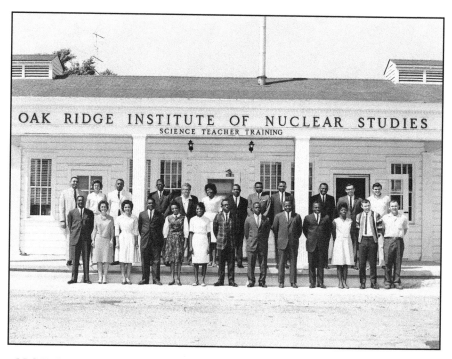

N.S.F. Summer Institute for College Teachers of Introductory Physics
Oak Ridge Institute of Nuclear Studies - 1964 (Author Collection)

VANDERBILT UNIVERSITY

SUMMER INSTITUTE ON DEVELOPMENTS IN MODERN PHYSICS

Certificate

This is to certify that

J. D. Oliver

has successfully completed the National Science Foundation
Summer Institute on Developments in Modern Physics
held at Vanderbilt University June 13-August 6, 1966.

D Kotelchuck

DIRECTOR

**Vanderbilt University Summer Institute on Developments
in Modern Physics – 1966 (Author Collection)**

Chapter 6

Cubicles and Punch Cards

Hiring and work at NASA complex—1969–1982;
information about space projects from the period,
launch pad tragedy; working at same location
with twin brother; professional relationships.

In 1969, the Apollo 11 mission was a success when the first man, Neil Armstrong, walked on the moon. Fifty years later, in 2019, our nation celebrated that major accomplishment in the space program. I also had reason to celebrate because A.D. and I both started working at Lockheed Electronics at the Johnson Space Center that same year.

Walking into the corporate work environment was a totally new experience for A.D. and me. We had spent the first eight years of our professional careers in the academic world, and here we were in the corporate world of work. The personnel director, Winston Johnson, who was also the Equal Employment Opportunity Commission

(EEOC) representative at Lockheed, was the staff person who got us on board and kept A.D. and me together in the same department. He guided and welcomed us to the company, helping us get settled into our new work environment. One of the first things we had to do was get security clearance which would give us approval to go onto the NASA site because Lockheed, a subcontractor, was off-site. This process took a few months because of all the verification involved, but we were already working while the clearance was being processed.

We were hired in January 1969 - the first African Americans hired as scientific programmers at Lockheed. In June of that year, Elnora Flewellen was hired. She was a graduate of Southern University, where A.D. and I once taught, but we did not know her nor was she in any of our classes. Melvin White, a senior programmer, was also hired around the same time. That made us the only four African Americans in our division at Lockheed—a momentous time!

The drive to Johnson Space Center from our homes in Houston was less than an hour. We were driving opposite of traffic that was coming into downtown Houston. A.D. and I carpooled together, and later, Elnora and Melvin joined us. We had a designated meeting place and took turns driving. It really saved wear and tear on our respective cars. A.D. and I both had Volkswagens. My VW was beige and his was red. There were some lively conversations on those trips to the Space Center!

There were other African Americans working on-site for NASA around that time. Often, there was some confusion where people worked at Johnson Space Center. NASA is considered on-site and all subcontractors, such as Lockheed Electronics and others, are considered off-site. We knew some of the African Americans at NASA because they were members of Wheeler Avenue Baptist Church. Julius Mayhorn - who lived in my neighborhood, Chuck Hoskins, Bob Ligon, Carrington Stewart (Carolyne's cousin), Bailey Davis, and George Keys were all church members. Others included Joseph

Atkins, Heibert Epps, who served on my advisory committee when I went to work at Prairie View, and Ken Martindale, who later worked with me on the software engineering initiative at Prairie View.

A.D. and I felt we were prepared for the job at Lockheed. All the years of teaching and studying math and science in National Science Foundation summer institutes at various universities had prepared us for our step into the corporate world. We had the same job, did the same kind of work, and were in the same building. We weren't ever separated and were treated well. We were introduced to scientists and other staff members and didn't experience any kind of resistance or problems. After seeing the movie *Hidden Figures*, I reflected on my time working in the space program and realized NASA and its subcontractors were following civil rights guidelines set by the federal government. Salary was about $10,000 a year, which was nice money at that time. When I left the educational system to take this job, I was making about $6,000 a year. It was a big jump in pay.

There were a lot of people working for Lockheed. Some worked in operations, running computers, and some worked as programmers. A.D. and I were part of a scientific programming staff that consisted of about 100 people—a decent-sized staff of mostly men and very few women. A lot of them came from the larger universities in different parts of the country—MIT, University of Texas, Texas A&M. We were all in cubicles. I sat on one side, and another employee sat on the other side. We had Univac machines to run programs and create code. Univac was a big, boxy machine similar to the IBM machine in *Hidden Figures*.

We handled programming that supported the Apollo and Space Shuttle programs. The work for the first Apollo moon shot had already been done when we were hired, but we worked on later Apollo missions. Although not aware at the time, I later learned that Project Apollo was NASA's third human spaceflight program and landed men on the moon from 1969 to 1972. I also learned that NASA was established during the Dwight Eisenhower administration, and the Apollo program, known as Project Apollo, was conceived during his administration. It was the Apollo program that was dedicated to achieving the national goal set by President Kennedy of landing a man on the moon by the end of the sixties. And they did!

It was interesting to note that two Texas-born presidents of the United States were responsible for the establishment and naming of the NASA Johnson Space Center. President Dwight Eisenhower, under whose administration NASA was established (1958), was raised in Kansas but born in Denison, Texas. I would call him a native Texan! The Johnson Space Center, originally named the Manned Spacecraft Center, was later renamed (1973) the Johnson Space Center in honor of President Johnson, who was born and raised in Stonewall, Texas. A native Texan! Now my brother and I were working at the NASA Johnson Space Center. Made me proud to be a Texan!

We wrote software programs using FORTRAN and Assembly Languages according to our assigned projects from designs that engineers had developed. The software programs consisted of a main program, supporting subroutines, and test data. We coded software programs in FORTRAN and/or Assembly Language on coding sheets, and the software programs were keyed in or punched on card decks by the typing pool group (as in *Hidden Figures*) and delivered back to us. The card decks matched what we coded and corresponded to the code that the IBM 7094 mainframe computers could interpret and/or read.

The card deck software programs were set up as specific jobs (the job control language identified each software program), then delivered to the computer labs for execution (preliminary testing) of the software programs we developed from a design. The turn-around time was usually one run per day, if you were lucky and submitted your job before noon. The cycle was repeated until all coding and diagnostic errors were resolved. In order to meet the completion schedule, and to save time, minor coding errors were corrected by the programmers who knew how to operate the keypunch machine without sending corrections back to us. After the coding and testing process was completed, we documented our assignments.

Every morning, we checked the box to see if the program we had worked on the day before had run through the computer. If it didn't run, we had to rework it and fix the error. If it did run and gave the correct solution, we moved on to the next task. Sometimes there would be two or three tasks to work on in a three-hour period.

I worked on five different projects in a ten-year span at Lockheed. These were non-real-time projects with a lot of testing. Each day I relied on my mathematical and scientific ability, using punch cards and the 029 Key Punch, the standard machine. We would work on calculations in our cubicles and then take the punch cards into the computer room.

Sometimes we had to wait until our coworker finished because we didn't have that many machines. Different people were working on various projects, so if you walked in and a coworker was already at the 029, you had to wait. Each of us had a big box of cards and we would go into the room, key in our employee identification code, and then type instructions on the card. It was a slow process. We would put the completed cards in a rack in the machine room. Another person would come in, pick up those cards, and carry them back to building 12—the NASA computer data processing center.

If there was an error, either in the calculations or instructions, the machine would show an error message. The computer operators would look at the ID code and bring back the program listing and the cards with the mistake to the assigned person. Then we would go back through those calculations again. We didn't have to redo all the cards, just the ones that had mistakes. We used Assembly Language to find the errors. Sometimes it took a few minutes and sometimes it would take a while. If you left off a period when typing the instructions, for instance, that error was quickly found, but calculation errors in the program might take some time. This was called debugging the program. Go through and find the errors. Sometimes the errors might pop right out at you; sometimes they wouldn't.

There was an evolution of IBM's keypunch system, and it seemed like every other year there were new variations on that system. They were making a lot of strides and changing the 029 system. A.D. and I had to keep up with the changes, but there was not a whole lot of training. There were consistent upgrades, but we had the basics and used our manuals. The manual would have some material that was in Assembly Language, but most times not, and it wasn't so drastic that we couldn't follow the progression. NASA got rid of the punch-card system while we were there and installed computer terminals in different locations over the site for our access.

A typical workday meant A.D. and I would arrive about 7:50 a.m. and start work at 8 a.m. We worked until 5 p.m. with one hour for lunch. We had to be on time to dedicate a full day of work. Lunch was at the same time every day—noon. I would either bring my lunch or go out and eat. There were lots of places for lunch around the Johnson Space Center. A.D. and I would sometimes go out to lunch in a nearby town—Webster. The restaurant there served the food we liked: mashed potatoes, gravy, and that sort of thing.

The people were welcoming to us in the restaurants and businesses around the Space Center. Perhaps our attire was an indication we were employed by NASA or one of the subcontractors—we had to wear a shirt and tie with a jacket and our security badge. Couldn't get on-site without a badge, so we had to make sure that it was visible at all times.

A.D. and I were fortunate because President Kennedy passed a decree in 1961 that banned segregation in the federal government and federal contractors. There were not any conversations on the job regarding the difficult subject of race relations or what was going on in society at that time. We just went along with our day and didn't say anything, not even in the lunchroom. Talk would be about sports and things like that, especially the Dallas Cowboys. I was a fan when Roger Staubach was the quarterback and Tom Landry was the coach.

While I was working at Lockheed in the late sixties and early seventies, there was a lot of fallout from the civil rights movement of the mid-sixties. But we never touched on those subjects, and didn't have any kind of society-related conversations with coworkers. We did our work, took a lunch, and went home. Sometimes we would go out with coworkers. They would have crab boils, Christmas parties, and family activities, but we never did get into discussions about what was going on in the world in politics or religion. We never talked about anything like that. When one employee would leave the company, we would go out to a luncheon as a group. We never had any problems.

My title changed several times while I was at Lockheed those ten years—from 1969 to 1979. I started out as a scientific programmer, then moved up to data systems analyst. When I started at Lockheed, man had not yet landed on the moon—that happened later in the year. The space program began to really advance after I began working at Lockheed. NASA began working on a space station and the space shuttle program.

In 1975, A.D. went over to McDonnell Douglas. The salary was better, and he had a more flexible work schedule that allowed him to follow his dream and start a business in the Clear Lake area. While he was at McDonnell Douglas, we continued to carpool because we were both in the same main complex but in different buildings. We lived next door to one another in Houston and still saw each other every morning and every evening.

The NASA complex was huge, with several companies that were contractors and subcontractors. IBM was one of the companies that had a big presence at Johnson Space Center. General Electric, TRW, Raytheon, Singer-Link, and Boeing were all major players. It was booming out there. There were thousands of people employed across the complex. A.D. could work at McDonnell and was close enough to run his business at the same time with the assistance of his wife, Helen. I stayed at Lockheed, not only because I was comfortable there, but I couldn't spend time on an outside business. The complexity of our projects was such that we had to remain focused because sometimes one project lasted an entire year. I stayed and became vested in the retirement program at Lockheed.

At one point, there was some talk of our going into business together. We all—Carolyne, A.D., Helen, and I—were going to move to Clear Lake and operate the business, but A.D. and Carolyne never did decide on a name for the company. Plus, Carolyne wanted her own business in typesetting and graphics in Houston, so that was that. A.D. received a loan from the Small Business Administration (SBA) and started taking on printing clients. We were supposed to consolidate Carolyne's company with his to have a family business, but it just didn't work out either. However, they did support each other by sharing clients.

I continued to have a quest for learning, so while working at Lockheed, I was attending classes and workshops on-site taught by professors from University of Houston-Clear Lake. Frank Barnes, one of my supervisors at Lockheed, suggested that instead of taking classes and workshops, I should enroll at UH-Clear Lake and work on a graduate degree in Computer Science. I followed his recommendation, completed my master's thesis—"Simulation of an Econometric Model Using an Interactive Computer System"—and graduated from UH-Clear Lake with a master's degree in the spring of 1980.

From Programming to Simulation

After ten years at Lockheed, I left in 1979 to work for Singer-Link. The opportunity to be more directly involved with space work was exactly what I was looking for. I provided programming, simulations, and documentation for the space shuttle, and handled support for the Test Case Usage Reporting System tied to the Space Vehicle Dynamic Simulation program. I participated in programming and documentation of the Memory Map Analyzer (MAZE) program, and used Assembly Language for that program. Sometimes I tested programs about a year before they were sent to the next stage to see if they were viable. Also, I provided support for the main program logic of the Aircraft Engineering Digital Simulation (AEDS) development task.

My work at Singer was mostly simulation work—testing our programs in the simulator to experience ascent, orbit, and descent. Although I was at Lockheed the longest and primarily did analysis work, it was all about simulation at Singer. The real-time simulation actually felt like flying the shuttle. I got that same feeling of flying when I tested the flight control navigation panel in the F-16 Falcon fighter jet flight simulator. Write the programs, then test them on the simulator...exhilarating work!

Testing of the F-16 flight control navigation panel was an example of collaboration between the aerospace companies. Although the F-16 fighter jet was built at the Lockheed Martin plant in Fort Worth, Texas, the simulation work for the flight control navigation panel was done at Singer-Link and not Lockheed. No doubt there was other collaboration that took place among the aerospace companies at NASA Johnson.

At Singer-Link, we worked in real-time simulation for the space shuttle. The programs we wrote to fly the space shuttle were tested in the simulator. We programmed the simulator with the equations for lifting off, orbiting the earth, and coming back. We used inertia measurement units (IMU), and there were phases called quaternion to measure speed, distance, velocity, and acceleration. All of this involved formulas and equations necessary to simulate the various phases of the space flight to see if it worked. When I was in the simulator, I could see what formulas worked, what didn't, then make adjustments. We had four general-purpose computers and one backup computer on the simulator. If something didn't work, we didn't scratch that formula, but went back and reworked it.

When our team received an assignment, we knew that it was going to be a part of a specific launch. The assignment would detail the plan to launch at a certain date in the future and individuals would be assigned to work one of the three phases. The assignment also listed a specific launch date to work toward. We had milestone deadlines and then we worked forward. For example, if a launch was scheduled in three years, we would back-calendar the project's starting point and then work toward that date.

I remember the launch of the first space shuttle—*Columbia*. This was an example of a scheduled launch. It was the first shuttle to fly in NASA's Space Shuttle program and was named STS-1(Space Transportation System-1). *Columbia* launched on April 12, 1981 and returned on April 14, orbiting the Earth thirty-six times. The shuttle had a two-man crew: mission commander John W. Young and pilot Robert L. Crippen.

The shuttle flights had three separate teams for the three aspects of the project—ascent, orbit, and descent, and there were certain codes related to each phase. I was on the ascent team, so my time in the simulator was to test the accuracy of our formulas and calculations for that phase.

By the time the general public saw the space launch on television and saw Mission Control out at Johnson Space Center, we had tested all those formulas. Mission Control was the center for all communications between Earth and the astronauts and was where in-flight decisions were made. At Mission Control, the team knew the expected results based on the simulations we had done. They would just watch the launch, or ascent phase, to ensure everything went forward according to our calculations. After the orbit and descent phase, those teams would come together and make corrections. Once the astronaut and the shuttle came back to Earth, we would recalculate the equations and make updates. There would be adjustments and fine-tuning.

Our mathematical and scientific training paid off as we set up and calculated applications and formulas. For example, we knew the basic formula for velocity, so it was easy to put data into the formula. We were constantly testing data. Even if it was a projection that had never been done before, the mathematical equations would tell us if it was going to work. That's where the simulations came in, to test the data. We would calculate, and engineers would confirm that the formula would work, so we put the data in that formula. When everything was applied, we would get the projected results—that's real-time simulation.

We weren't concerned about failure because if the formula did not work, we would correct it. We would compute velocity and distance. We knew what we were looking for to get the right results. The acceleration tells you how much power per square inch has to be applied in order to move to a certain point and beyond. Velocity has to include distance and the speed of time. So, if you know to get to the moon is a certain distance, then you have to compute how much velocity and acceleration would be needed to complete that distance. That's all part of the equation.

Engineers would calculate the distance to the moon and back according to the speed of light, and the formula would be based on that computation. The speed of light is 186,000 miles per second and from there you can figure out velocity. This would provide the speed it would take for a rocket to go a certain distance. Then we would develop the necessary formulas to calculate the pounds per square inch to launch. The speed of sound is a little different because air is a gas, and the speed of transmission is a small disturbance through a medium (NASA). It also depends on the type and temperature of the gas. This is why sometimes during a launch, the actual sound of the ascent takes a few minutes to be transmitted back to Earth and to human ears.

The entire distance the rocket traveled—ascent to descent—was controlled by teams at Johnson Space Center in Houston. All teams were working in the same building, but on different schedules. The schedules were set according to different applications. The simulators were in Building 5, and schedules were adjusted because all of the teams would use the same simulator. We used only one of the two simulators, and various teams did shift work to apply different applications and send the code over to program the simulator.

NASA and all its sub-contractors had security clearance. There were three levels of clearance—confidential, secret, and top secret. I had secret clearance, but that did not mean we could not talk about the project outside of the complex or outside of work. I never had top secret clearance, the highest level of security involving possible classified documentation, which would have stopped me from talking about critical parts of any project we were working on. We knew what to discuss and what to avoid if we were at lunch away from the complex or if we were at home and in social settings. Besides, most people wouldn't have known what we were talking about anyway, so it didn't matter a whole lot.

I didn't talk about Singer too much because most people thought the company only made sewing machines, but what they did not know is that the company did a lot in the area of technology, especially when I was there. Singer did some excellent work.

Space tragedies

Sometimes, even with the best calculations, there would be disaster. In 1967, three astronauts—Edward White, Virgil "Gus" Grissom, and Roger Chaffee—were killed in a fire on the launching pad for the Apollo 1 mission. I'm sure that team was broken-hearted at the loss of life on that horrible day, especially with all of the careful work that goes into a manned project. The Apollo 1 fire was an extreme case, but more than likely, the project wasn't ready to fly. A tragedy at that level would mean that a team would look even more closely into safety. By the time A.D. and I were on board at Lockheed, safety was strongly emphasized.

When there is a problem of that magnitude, the engineers and management get together, figure out what went wrong, then take steps to fix it. They start by going back to the formula end, see if there are any mistakes, and work their way forward. Then they go back to the liftoff team and start reviewing all the formulas involved at that point.

In 1986, President Ronald Reagan announced that an African American astronaut and a woman science teacher were members of the team to fly the next mission into space. The flight was scheduled for January 28, 1986—the coldest day in history that a shuttle had been launched. Seventy-three seconds into the flight, the space shuttle *Challenger* exploded, and seven astronauts lost their lives. Intensive investigation of that failed flight revealed the mission was doomed due to extreme weather and the failure of the aft joint seal in the right solid rocket booster. Administrators approved the flight to stay on schedule even though the weather was extremely cold. A.D. and I knew the African American astronaut, Ron McNair. He was the only one we knew who was lost in a space-related accident. We were hurt. The result of the *Challenger* disaster was that NASA grounded the Shuttle project for three years to install new safety measures, redesign the boosters, and take another look at launch processes. The tragedy set the space program back due to government reassessment and funding cuts.

All of the teams involved in a failed mission project rework everything. Failure was not an option because lives were at stake. After the *Challenger* tragedy, NASA was faced with a lot of complaints about the money being spent on space, especially since our society had so many problems that needed to be addressed here on Earth—hunger and poverty. There are about five different teams involved to get a project to the point of launch, and a lot of money is spent. But this was the Kennedy legacy since the Russians had beat the U.S. into space. President Kennedy wanted NASA to put a man on the moon and return him safely. After *Challenger*, we had to be extremely careful before sending another manned craft into space.

African American Astronauts

I knew of all the African American astronauts. Most of them were selected as astronauts after A.D. and I began working at Lockheed. I knew Ron McNair well because he was a member of our church (Wheeler Avenue Baptist Church) and had started a karate program there for the youths. His wife is still an active member at Wheeler, and Carolyne knows her. When the *Challenger* exploded, that was a terrible day. I was teaching at Prairie View when the news came through. It was awful, just awful. McNair was a graduate of North Carolina A&T and MIT (Massachusetts Institute of Technology). A great mind, great physicist, wonderful person. A tremendous loss.

Guion Bluford was the first African American to go into space. Bernard Harris, who, after serving as an astronaut, created a foundation and partnered with ExxonMobil to develop summer science camps and other STEM (Science, Technology, Engineering, and Math) programs for middle-school kids. His program is at Prairie View in partnership with the engineering college there. Frederick Gregory and Robert Satcher were other astronauts I knew of. I know

Charles Bolden, who flew four missions in space—two as a commander and two as a pilot. He, his wife, Carolyne and I were in an organization together and would see each other socially. Bolden was appointed by President Obama to become the director of NASA, taking the helm in 2009. He was military, graduated from the Naval Academy, was a major general in the Marines and retired. Bolden was a top-notch administrator. These astronauts are all retired now, but all left their mark on the space program.

Some of the women astronauts were Stephanie Wilson, Joan Higginbottom, and Sally Ride—the first woman to go into space. I vaguely knew Yvonne Cagle, but knew Mae Jemison, the first African American woman in space. She flew aboard the *Endeavor* on mission STS-47 and spent eight days in space. She had a business out at NASA at one time but has since retired from flying. All are great women in the industry.

The last space shuttle disaster was the *Columbia* (STS-107) on February 1, 2003. I was especially heart-broken over this disaster because I worked on the first flight *Columbia* took (STS-1) back in 1982. Space shuttle *Columbia* flew for twenty-one years. There was an African American on board, Michael Anderson, who was the payload commander. I didn't know Michael.

IBM 029 Keypunch System

ALT AWARD

J. D. OLIVER

The crews of the Approach and Landing Test Program are pleased to present you with this medallion in appreciation of your contribution to the successful ALT flights of the space shuttle orbiter "Enterprise".

Manned Flight Awareness

Lockheed Certificate of Appreciation for contributions to the Approach and Landing Test flights of the space shuttle "Enterprise" (Author Collection)

LINK FLIGHT SIMULATION DIVISION
OF THE SINGER COMPANY
HOUSTON OPERATIONS

Presents this certificate to

J. D. Oliver

in appreciation for your contribution to the success of the
F-16 Simulator Program.

David R. Zahler
Program Manager

David W. Lamar
Program Manager

Philip J. Anderson
General Manager, Houston Operations

Link Flight Simulator Award for contributions toward
the success of the F-16 Simulator Program
(Author Collection)

fiʀst shuttLe flight achievement awaʀ∂

'The crew of Columbia is pleased to present you with this medallion in appreciation of your contribution to the success of the First Manned Orbital Flight of the Space Shuttle.

J. D. OLIVER

NASA

MANNED FLIGHT AWARENESS

John Young   Bob Crippen

First Shuttle Flight Achievement Award from the
crew of Columbia (Author Collection)

The University of Houston at Clear Lake City

has conferred upon

J. D. Oliver

the degree of

Master of Science

with all the rights and privileges appertaining thereto.
In Witness Thereof, this diploma duly signed has been issued and the
seal of the University hereunto affixed.

Issued by the Board of Regents upon recommendation of the faculty at Houston, Texas,
on this thirteenth day of December, A.D. nineteen hundred and eighty.

Chairman of the Board of Regents

Charles E. Bishop
President

S.R. Neumann
Chancellor

Masters Degree – UH Clear Lake

Chapter 7

Academics and Academia

*Return to Prairie View; teaching and
developing the computer science program
and curriculum; financing the program;
NASA initiatives and creation of the Storefront.*

When I left Lockheed Electronics in 1979 to work for Singer-Link, for the first time I began doing real-time programming. This was the kind of challenging, yet enjoyable work I never dreamed I would do. But, in spite of the work's significance and excitement, and my time in corporate, there was still the desire to teach. The words of my aunt Callie continued to ring true in my heart: "As long as there are Black children, there will be a need for Black teachers."

During my third year at Singer, I was contacted by Dr. Edward Martin, dean of the College of Arts and Sciences at Prairie View A&M University (PV), to inquire if I was interested in coming to work there to build and direct a computer science program. I learned that Prairie View needed to build the program to be in compliance with the Texas Plan[1] that was part of a federal mandate, and they needed someone with the expertise and desire to make it happen. I felt this was my chance, and that my experiences in teaching at universities and working in the space arena would be valuable in fulfilling my dream to educate African American students. What better place to do that than at my alma mater?

After discussing the move with Carolyne, I resigned from Singer-Link and was hired in the fall of 1982 as assistant professor and director of the Computer Science Program at Prairie View. I could have stayed at Johnson Space Center and Singer-Link until I retired, but I chose to make the move. The pay for an assistant professor at Prairie View was a little less than what I was earning, but I wanted to do more, something different and more challenging. NASA was moving toward more work on the Space Station—more calculations, tedious work. But I continued to have a desire to teach.

My salary had increased over the years at Lockheed and Singer-Link, as my job descriptions changed and my responsibilities grew, but that didn't matter. I was ready for something more rewarding, to give back to my community in another way. I had savings and income from other sources, so I knew that my family and I would be okay.

Twenty-one years after my graduation from Prairie View A&M College, I was recruited back to build a computer science curriculum to be in compliance and to keep the university on pace with technology. An entire program was going to have to be built from the ground up, so I had to dedicate my time and effort to do it. It meant I would have to make some sacrifices to get the job done.

---

1   The Texas Plan was a proposal submitted in 1981 by Governor Williams Clements to the U.S. Department of Education's Office of Civil Rights (OCR) in response to an investigation between 1978 and 1980 of higher education in the state of Texas as a result of the *Adams v. Richardson* case which was filed by the NAACP in 1970 against the U.S. Department of Health, Education, and Welfare.

When I arrived at PV in '82, the computer science program was in the mathematics department of the College of Arts and Sciences with Dr. Frank Hawkins as department chair. The college was located in the Hobart Taylor Building. Earlier attempts had been made to build a computer science program, but the curriculum was virtually nonexistent. I reviewed copies of letters and memos dated as far back as August 1967 in which then President A. I. Thomas had requested recommendations from the math department on building a curriculum to implement a computer science program. The program was to be created right away and would be based on what was outlined in the March 1968 publication from the Association of Computing Machinery called *Curriculum '68*. When I arrived, the only thing that existed was an office and an empty laboratory assigned to computer science.

Students were enrolled in a computer option course in the math department because there was no computer science program. However, the university was mandated to have Bachelor of Science (B.S.) degrees in Computer Science (CS), and Computer Technology initiated in the fall of '83. Dr. Ivory V. Nelson, interim president at the time, was supportive and wanted to move forward aggressively in building these programs. My time was spent collecting information and designing a curriculum to have a CS program ready for approval by the Coordinating Board in the Spring 1983 semester so computer science classes could start in the fall of that year. With the assistance of Norman Hunter, who was hired about the same time as I to be the Information Systems person, and of Charles Coats, who was my administrative assistant, we had much work to do.

My commute time to PV from Houston was a little over an hour each way—two hours—time that I could have spent working on the curriculum. After talking it over with Carolyne, I decided to move closer to the university. This was going to be the first time ever I lived away from my family. Jay had just started first grade, so this was a big adjustment for all of us. I settled in the first year and lived near the university in a small apartment in Hempstead. This move allowed me to work as late as I needed on campus, grab dinner, and continue working in my apartment.

Although I came home on the weekends, my time was mostly spent building the curriculum on our dining room table. Carolyne did as much as she could to ensure we had family interaction during the weekends. We always went to church and had dinner together. We attended a few social events just to have some together "down time" when we could. I remember Carolyne setting Jay at the table with me to do his homework while I worked on building the program—creating some semblance of father-son time. I was on a tight schedule to submit a proposal to the Texas A&M University System for approval, but tried to give our family some time and attention. Jay was a Cub Scout in Troop 242 at our church, so some of my time on Saturdays was spent with him at Scout meetings and activities.

Computer Science was a four-year degree program, and the full outline and curriculum for the new degree granting program had to be submitted by February 1983, approved, and in place by the fall of the same year. After about a year of coming home only on weekends, I felt I needed to be around to help raise our son, so I gave up living in Hempstead and came home every evening, still working right on our dining table. I continued my research and detailing the curriculum, although I had no idea how many students were going be in the classes. The mandate was to have 170 students enrolled in five years. Additionally, my performance evaluation was going to be based on success in meeting the objectives in building the program.

Commuting to and from Prairie View remained a challenge. I sought other means of transportation other than driving daily. There was a commuter van that picked up university personnel who lived in Houston and transported them to campus. Those who rode the van met around 7:00 a.m. in the parking lot off Hollister Road and

Highway 290. The van left the campus every day at 5:00 p.m. This did work for me briefly, but after the first computer science classes started in fall '83, I realized I needed to be there as much as possible to meet students' needs and tweak the program. I could not continue to ride the van and had to seek other commuter arrangements. I tried to carpool with Karen Charleston, one of the PV employees who lived near me. We would alternate driving weeks, but then again, I was at the mercy of someone else's schedule. None of the carpooling options worked for me, so I ended up driving to work every day. At least I could arrive as early and stay as late as I needed to get the work done.

There were twenty-nine state schools and nine private schools in Texas in 1982 with degree programs in computer science, but Prairie View was not one of them. The nearest institution offering a similar program was the Texas A&M System flagship school, Texas A&M University in College Station, located forty-five miles north of Prairie View. PV's administration was anxious for the program to start, but because of budgetary constraints, it was somewhat difficult to build the infrastructure and secure the necessary equipment.

Technology was evolving and I thought a five-year plan would work best. My approach was to set up the first program, then revisit at the four-year mark to plan further. Computer science was a new discipline and we wanted to prepare our students for the changes that were coming. Computers at Prairie View were almost nonexistent at the time. Everything was handwritten or done on a typewriter. There weren't even computers in the classroom. The College of Business had computer-related courses, but it was just data processing. The university was still doing their payroll manually. Back then, computers were big and bulky with vacuum tubes, and were set up in rooms. We had a long way to go.

Early development

When it came to politics, Prairie View was like any other university in the country. A change in the administration, especially at the presidential level, meant changes could be expected in academic offerings and in other institutional areas to support that leader's vision. The same held true with Dr. Percy A. Pierre, who became PV's fourth president in spring 1983. Dr. Pierre ushered in his vision for the university, but one thing did not change—he remained focused on the mandate required by the Texas Plan to have a CS program ready by that fall.

We met the deadline and I taught the first Computer Science class in the fall of 1983. I had ordered the books and brought in a lot of supplemental reading material that I requested from Association for Computing Machinery (ACM). I paid for copying materials to be used in the class since my operating budget was so small. I used a lot of my own money to buy books, paper, pens, and office supplies. I wanted to help the university catch up with other institutions in this field, so I self-funded small items for a while. Students were challenged since most didn't have calculators, so all their calculations were on paper. I believed students were stronger mathematically when they were not using calculators. They had to mentally calculate mathematical problems even though they could complete their assignments faster with a tool. Engineering students who enrolled in computer science used the book and a slide rule, a critical tool for their curriculum.

I wasn't nervous about teaching at the college level because I had been in classrooms before, giving me the necessary confidence to handle students. This was a new curriculum that I was developing while I was teaching, so there was a little bit of pressure, but I knew what the students needed to learn: computer languages, operating systems, and data structure.

When Dr. Pierre took the helm at Prairie View, I was unaware of the changes taking place within the Texas Legislature that ultimately impacted funding at the university. Prairie View had long been denied access to the Permanent University Funds (PUF), which was a permanent endowment established in 1876 to fund higher education in the state of Texas.[2] With the support of advocates and legislators, this was changing and was good news for Prairie View and for the growth of all of its academic programs.

After Dr. Pierre reorganized some of the academic programs, the CS program was transferred to the Engineering Technology Department located in the newly created College of Applied Science and Engineering Technology, and Dr. Hakumat Israni was named dean of that college. Creating a new college to include the departments of electrical engineering technology, mechanical engineering technology, and the computer science program showed that the university was committed to moving into the world of technology.

I was asked to assist in building a computer engineering technology curriculum in the new college as well as continue coordinating the CS program that was now operating as a department. In fact, we were building faculty to specifically help design, manage and plan courses rather than just identifying a collection of courses that could lead to a CS degree or certificate. We behaved more like a department and I was treated as a department head and not just a program coordinator. Dr. David Kirkpatrick, the engineering technology department head, and I worked together to build the new technology

---

2   Although PV had been in existence since 1878 and was established as the Agricultural and Mechanical College of Texas for Colored Youth managed by the Agricultural College of Bryan (Texas A&M University) board of directors, it had never benefitted from the Permanent University Fund (PUF) which was a perpetual endowment established in 1876 to fund higher education in Texas. With the support of university advocates and legislators, the Texas Legislature proposed a constitutional amendment in 1983 to restructure the PUF to include Prairie View and declared the university to be "an institution of the first class" under the governing board of the A&M University System. Additionally, in January 1985, the Texas A&M University Board of Regents responded to a 1984 Constitutional Amendment stating its intention that Prairie View was to be nationally recognized in education and research. This meant that PV would receive its share of the Available University Fund (AUF), which is a portion of the returns from the PUF annually distributed to the Texas A&M and University of Texas systems.

curriculum, but I never lost focus on shaping the computer science program. I continued to build the CS curriculum based on the ACM model that gave requirements and updates every ten years and was the road map for building and maintaining a program. This curriculum was also used for accreditation purposes.

Prairie View was mandated to start six new degree programs by the fall of 1983. This was in accordance with the 1983 Texas Plan for Equal Educational Opportunity approved by the Department of Education as a result of the *Adams v. Richardson* case filed in 1970 against the U.S. Department of Health, Education, and Welfare by the NAACP.[3] However, only two were successful: Computer Science and Computer Engineering Technology.

Funding Computer Science

As with all academic programs, the university provided basic funding for the CS program, but I applied for grants to buy equipment and continue building out the program. Corporate support began early. One of my earliest grants came in 1984 when IBM donated twenty-five computers—the first PCs donated to the program.

IBM's gift was a major accomplishment. The equipment was donated through writing proposals and making contacts that year. The computers—big, bulky, boxy-looking PCs—were square and white. Those PCs were self-contained and not connected to any network. Getting those computers allowed students to get hands-on experience learning programming and Assembly Language.

More corporate backing came in 1989, when AT&T Bell

---

3   The celebrated *Adams v. Richardson* case addressed the dismantling of dual systems of public higher education that existed well after the passage of the Civil Rights Act of 1964, which mandated, among other benefits to black Americans, the removal of racial discrimination in education. The Department of Health, Education, and Welfare found that ten states still had segregated higher education systems during the period of January 1969 until February 1970. The mandate referred to those public colleges that received federal funds. HEW required each state to submit a desegregation plan. The case was heard in the U.S. Court of Appeals for the District of Columbia, June 12, 1973. This case had a positive impact on public and private black colleges in several areas and underscored the need for their continued existence.

Laboratories donated computer equipment worth $264,000. Prairie View was one of thirteen universities nationwide to receive a gift from AT&T that year. The hardware, software, and training helped our students learn C-programming, and later, a popular language called C++. Also, we began teaching UNIX. AT&T's corporate relations sent visiting professors to the lab and gave us hardware. AT&T was impressed with the quality of our proposal and the involvement of faculty and students in the CS program. AT&T sent Iyengar "Ravi" Ravindra, one of our professors, to a workshop in New Orleans to learn the UNIX operating system and C programming language. Although we were a young program, AT&T had developed a strong recruiting relationship with PV, which improved our chances for being funded.

I was also busy building faculty during this time. Ravi and Dr. Kwang Paick transferred to Computer Science from the Math Department. Then I hired two professors—Dr. Thembavani Gopalakrishan and Dr. Shakir Safwat. Myrtle Thompkins, who was a professor in Industrial Education, joined our staff when that department was merged with the College of Applied Sciences. That gave us a total of six faculty, including myself. Industry professionals, also known as "loan professors," were recruited to teach some classes. The formal loan program, which was an agreement fostered through our industry connections, enabled us to get more loan professors from AT&T, IBM, and Boeing. Over the years, as faculty continued to grow and evolve, I needed to hire a computer technician to help maintain department computers. Chris Galvez, a computer science graduate who had completed his military obligation with the US Navy, was the perfect fit and was hired.

The objective was to build a strong program with small classes so I could work one-on-one with students. Since I was using the ACM model to build the curriculum, and wanted to remain connected to ACM on all levels, we started an ACM student chapter in 1991 at Prairie View. The next year, four students from our ACM chapter - Robert Provencal, Donald Richardson, Ram Anad, and Tom Chikoore, traveled to Texas Tech University to compete in the 18th Annual Association of Computing Machinery South Central Region International Collegiate Programming Contest. These were senior computer science honor students and they did quite well. Fifty-six teams from thirty-four schools in the region participated. Students from Rice University won the competition since they had an established computer science curriculum, but our students weren't intimidated and held their own.

I had great students during that time—Charles Hardnett, Cynthia Lester, Ralphael Wilson are some that stand out in my mind. Charles went to Georgia Tech, earned a doctorate in computer science, and was hired at Spelman College in Atlanta. Cynthia obtained her doctorate from the University of Alabama and became chair of the Computer Science Department at Tuskegee University in Alabama. She moved on to the corporate world, then back to academics. She became associate dean and chair of the Computer Science and Engineering Department at Georgia State University. Ralphael went to Nortel Network Systems and came back to support the department at PV by spearheading a major corporate gift and serving on the CS Advisory Board. These students, and so many others, made me proud.

Computer science now is less math oriented. In the early days, it was loaded with math and writing code—COBOL, FORTRAN, C, and C++. All the languages involve writing code. The curriculum started out with Computer Science basics and moved into FORTRAN. Computer Science students had to take differential calculus, integral calculus, numerical analysis, and differential equations. These weren't elective courses at that time. Most of the students entered Prairie View as math majors and then switched to Computer Science.

The CS program was built by word of mouth, and we gained students by working with the Prairie View recruitment staff. We would go to college fairs, talk about the program, and distribute brochures. Many of the high schools didn't have any type of computer curriculum, so we were recruiting students with no prior CS knowledge. They didn't have anything that piqued their interest in computer science before we got there, so this was all new to most of them. Students would come to the campus and didn't even know how to turn on the computer, but by the time they graduated, they were computer literate.

Industry funding would be used to buy computers, the same equipment that major universities used. Corporate funds were increasing, and those dollars went straight into my budget. However, research money or funding from government grants and proposals had indirect costs, where the principal investigator (PI) receives a percentage. Funding from government grants was disbursed through the university's research and sponsored programs office. All the funds I received from the corporate world went directly into the program for operations.

I was writing papers for publication, producing proposals, and looking for funding during the summer. External support was critical to run a good program in computer science. I was also conducting research on building the curriculum and keeping up with trends in the industry. IBM was coming out with new trends every six months for a while, and we would have to keep up. There was new information coming in the mail—magazines discussing new trends in the computer industry—then we would have to learn whatever that was, absorb it, and be prepared to change the curriculum. New computer language kept coming down the pike, so we had to review and learn every aspect to teach our students.

We altered the curriculum several times. Every ten years there was new material that came out of ACM. We started teaching UNIX because it had become popular. When AT&T gave us their equipment, the company emphasized teaching UNIX, C, and C++. The industry went to JAVA in 1990.

We shared our computer equipment and knowledge with the university. We trained administrators on IBM PCs and offered a computer introduction course with the four major applications: Word, Excel, Access, and PowerPoint. When we received equipment donations, our program gave a computer to the deans and got them started with training. I had an advisory committee with about ten people from industry—management people who kept us informed. Two advisory board members who started with us and who continue to serve today are Heibert Epps with NASA and Pearl Wright, a minority woman-owned subcontractor.

Students would become interns in industry in the summer and return to campus, updating us on the projects they worked on and what trends were evolving. We were getting information from everywhere—Apple, Microsoft, etc. All of their programs were being developed and rolled out fast. The advisory committee was helping us find money and learn about innovations. They provided insight on what courses we should teach and what we should drop, helped us with internships and placing our students in careers. Some of our students had five or six job offers upon graduation.

Change in leadership

The university experienced another change in leadership as the computer science program continued to grow. Lt. General Julius W. Becton became the fifth president of the university in 1989. I felt good about General Becton becoming president because of his prior association with Prairie View. He was a graduate of the university, taught ROTC there, and served in the military with many PV ROTC graduates, many of whom became generals. He was well known prior to his arrival.

Carolyne and A.D. both joined me on campus for President Becton's Inaugural Ceremony. All activities took place during Homecoming Week, creating a festive atmosphere. It was a great day for the university because General Colin Powell, a close friend of General Becton, was the keynote speaker. General Powell had been appointed by President George H.W. Bush to serve as chairman of the Joint Chiefs of Staff, and was the first African American and the youngest general to serve in that capacity. The pomp and circumstance of that inauguration involving two military generals was unforgettable. There was military representation from Fort Hood, and all of the Army and Navy ROTC students were on parade. Prairie View could boast about a host of military generals who had graduated from the university.

It was a great day for me because it was the first time in many years that my brother had visited the campus. His presence brought back memories of the days when he and I walked across campus together—going to class and the dining hall, social activities, and being known as the "Coke guys." We met some of my students and, of course, they expressed amazement when they saw us together because none of them knew I had a twin.

One of President Becton's goals was to make the university fiscally sound. He made some bold moves to balance the budget by suspending the athletic program—including football. It seemed athletics was draining the university coffers, and limiting academic support. Eliminating athletics did not set well with the alumni, but it was a move Becton had to make to get PV's finances in order. His actions were critical to redirect funding to sustain the university and support academic programs. A bigger computer science budget meant we could consider moving to the next stage of program development—getting accredited and becoming a department. Becton was a strong supporter of the CS program. Since we were moving forward in meeting the Texas Plan mandate of having 170 students in the program within ten years, it seemed only natural that the next step was to get the program accredited.

During my tenure as a professor at Prairie View, I learned that for an academic program to be successful, support must come from the top down. The president must be committed, as well as the vice president of academic affairs (provost), the academic deans, faculty, and students. Also, the program must be relevant to the university's mission and the vision of its leaders. Technology was moving fast in the 1990s, and Prairie View had to catch up to be relevant and prepare students for the fast-paced technological society. PV also had to take its academic place and be recognized as an intricate part of the Texas A&M University System. The CS program had that level of support.

When Dr. Pierre became president, his background in engineering helped him understand and create a vision in computer education. He began moving the university into the technology age. President Becton's vision was continuing the university's mission through sound financial practices, and this meant that funding would be available to support all academic programs, and most especially important for me, computer science.

Dean Israni was there to support my steps to strengthen computer science and the critical move toward accreditation. Without hesitation, he approved the funding and hiring of additional faculty and equipment purchases—anything I needed. We had met the Office of Civil Rights desegregation plans by creating the program and enrolling the requisite number of students, and if the accreditation push went well, it would be a major accomplishment for the university and our students.

Final push for accreditation

In early 1990, I recommended to Dean Israni that we apply for accreditation for the Computer Science program during the 1991–92 academic year. This required submitting a proposal to the Computer Science Accreditation Commission (CSAC) of the Computing Sciences Accreditation Board (CSAB). I knew the university would have to provide resources and upgrades, hire faculty, and expand library holdings for computer science, but I felt that the administrative climate was right to make this happen. We received the formal invitation from CSAC in November 1990 to submit the program for evaluation. This gave us approximately one year to prepare for the visit.

There was a lot of preparation work to be done because it was the first time for this curriculum. We had to complete a comprehensive self-study that required us to meet seventy-two standards focusing on institutional environment for the computer science program and its characteristics in the areas of program design, faculty, curriculum, laboratory and computing resources, students, and institutional support. We had to prepare exhibits of texts, syllabi, assignments, and graded examples of student work of good, average, and poor quality, and had to show to the accreditation board the success of our graduates.

The faculty and I had our hands full. They had full teaching loads and assisted with preparation wherever they could, and I had administrative duties, teaching and leading the accreditation preparation. We needed assistance with collecting information for the exhibits and ensuring that deadlines would be met. Dr. Anil Kumar, a professor and senior faculty in engineering, joined us in this effort. However with his teaching load, we still needed additional help. So I turned again to corporate for support. This time I found Algie Armstead, a PV engineering graduate who was working at McDonnell Douglas. He joined us as a loan professor and worked to prepare exhibits and other display materials, staying with us until the accreditation process was completed. Algie was a godsend, taking ownership of the exhibits to ensure that his alma mater delivered a good showing to the board. We appreciated his dedication and hard work. Daniel Yochim, another great fit for our team, was on loan to us from IBM. We requested that his professorship assignment be extended through the accreditation process to shore up the teaching load of faculty until permanent faculty could be hired.

During this time, Carolyne was hired by the College of Engineering as assistant to the dean. This was a tremendous help to me since we could ride to work together. Driving that two-hour commute was a challenge for me, but Carolyne was a better driver and enjoyed being behind the wheel. The biggest driving problem in the mornings was the congested traffic around the Galleria area on the 610 Loop in Houston. The evening commute back to Houston was a lot easier because we missed the traffic since we both stayed late. Carolyne drove in the mornings and I drove back in the evenings. This was our "together" time, giving us the opportunity to talk about the happenings on the campus that day. It allowed me the time to talk through the accreditation process and get her input. We would have a Snapple drink and eat peanut butter crackers as we drove back, wound down, and prepared to shift into home mode.

My mother-in-law, Ruby, whom I also called Mother, lived with us and helped take care of Jay and our home by handling chores and cooking so that Carolyne would not have so much to do when we got home. Mother was a Christian woman, and the love and care she gave us reminded me so much of my own mother. She had some break-ins to her home just before she retired from work as secretary to the Fort Bend County Extension Office, so we insisted that she move in with us for her own protection. This was to be a temporary move, but once she moved in, we all wanted her to stay. Jay was in middle school at the time, so this worked out perfectly for all of us. She was there when he came home from school and was his "go to" person when Carolyne and I were not available. As it turned out, she was his "go to" person even when we were available. There is nothing like the grandparent-grandchild bond! Her presence in our home was a blessing. Later, Carolyne and I decided that picking up dinner would benefit all of us. Family support made a huge difference!

We were ready for the accreditation team by Fall 1991. The visit was scheduled for November 3rd through 5th. The group arrived on Sunday evening, the 3rd, and began reviewing materials. They came to the campus first thing Monday morning to meet with university administrators—first, the president and provost, then on to interview the dean and faculty of the Computer Science program and review the exhibits and display materials, thanks to Algie. We hosted a reception Monday evening for the accreditation team, the university president, provost, and other senior administrators. The team met with Dean Israni on Tuesday morning to discuss their preliminary findings, and then they were off.

It was a whirlwind trip. We had to be on our toes to provide details when answering pointed questions about the program. I was upbeat about our chances because we had done all of the critical work in preparation and thoroughly understood our program. It was a hurry-up-and-wait situation because we would not hear the results of the team's findings until Spring 1992.

Dr. Israni received a response from the CSAB Commission in March 1992. There was one major deficit—the need for an additional faculty member with a doctorate degree. The other issues were minor and could easily be corrected. President Becton approved Dr. Israni's request for a new faculty member, and we prepared a follow-up report once the other deficits were corrected.

While we awaited the accreditation board's final decision, I continued to build partnerships, solicit corporate support, and recruit students, doing all that I could to advance our program. I traveled to California in the spring of '92 to attend a Supercomputer Workshop sponsored by the National Energy Research Supercomputer Center at Lawrence Livermore National Laboratory. The focus was on hosting workshops to train local math and science teachers on how to access and utilize the National Education Supercomputer (NES). I believed that the more I could engage area high school teachers and introduce them to the computing world, the better we could boost recruitment and prepare more students to enter our program at PV.

Dr. Israni received advance notice that our computer science program had been accredited on July 1, 1992. He was notified right after the CSAC held its annual meeting in Dallas in late June. This preceded the official notification that would be sent to President Becton by Dr. Joseph Turner, president of the Computer Science Accrediting Board. We learned that our program had been accredited for three years, the maximum for a new initiative. What an accomplishment! We began receiving congratulatory letters from everywhere, including Dr. Herbert H. Richardson, then chancellor of the Texas A&M University System, as well as other deans and department heads from Texas A&M. One comment was striking: "Achieving such an accreditation under any circumstances is a noteworthy achievement. However, succeeding in receiving CSAC accreditation within ten years of a program's implementation is extraordinary." So, there we were—I was hired in 1982 to build a computer science program and ten years later, we were accredited for three years on our first attempt. It was a great reward for all of the work and sacrifice, and that said it all for me. This accomplishment made me feel as though I was on top of the world.

Every career step led to this moment: teaching—both in secondary and higher education—attending National Science Foundation (NSF)-sponsored math and science seminar sessions and workshops around the country, and the scientific programming and space simulation work I did at the Johnson Space Center. All of this contributed to my qualifications to build a solid computer science program at Prairie View. This was a first-time discipline, and once accredited, it's a lot easier to get funding. We received more good news as we grew.

The second time we were up for accreditation in 1995, we were approved for the maximum six years!

Accreditation could not have been more critical to the computer science program and the university at that time. To put things in perspective, there were 117 Historically Black Colleges and Universities (HBCUs) in the country. Only forty offered a bachelor's degree in computer science, and of the forty, only six had accredited CS programs—Howard University, Hampton University, Southern University at Baton Rouge, Jackson State University, Norfolk University, and Prairie View.

According to the Texas Higher Education Coordinating Board, there were a total of fifty computer science programs in Texas in 1992 and only six were accredited—University of Houston–University Park, University of Texas at El Paso, University of North Texas, Baylor University, Texas Christian University, and Prairie View. Accreditation meant that graduates could get top jobs because their degrees carried more weight in the corporate world since their studies had met certain guidelines and requirements. Prairie View's computer science program was the first in the Texas A&M System to be accredited—PV's program was designated in 1992, and Texas A&M in College Station received their designation in 1993. This achievement really put Prairie View on the map. We beat the big boys!

Words could not describe the excitement felt throughout the program. While we celebrated our accomplishment in every way possible, we were still a program and not a department. We were already being referred to as the "computer science department" and I functioned as a "department head." Officially, we were a program, and I was the program coordinator, so a lot had to change.

Another major step loomed. The computer science program needed to become a department. This designation would have an even stronger appeal to industry and our students, and would move the university forward in its quest for recognition in the technological world. It would mean that Prairie View had gone above and beyond the Texas Plan mandate with the requisite number of graduates and was an accredited department in a recognized college—Applied Sciences and Engineering Technology.

The wheels for computer science becoming a department were put in motion by Provost Flossie Byrd. President Becton gave his approval to move forward, and the Coordinating Board approved Prairie View's request to create a Computer Science Department on October 28, 1993. There it was—in a little over a year, from June 1992 to October 1993, we became an accredited program and a department. I was thankful and blessed beyond measure to have accomplished all the major objectives set when I arrived as program coordinator in 1982. The Lord was with me.

Curriculum success and more corporate support

When Carolyne was initially hired in the engineering department in the spring of '91, her primary responsibility was student recruitment and managing the Engineering Concepts Institute (ECI), a summer bridge program for incoming freshman engineering majors. The program was a success, so at the end of the summer, she applied for and was hired as assistant to the dean of Engineering. She worked with the interim dean, Marshall Brown, until the end of the fall 1991 semester when John Foster was hired as the engineering dean. Dr. Foster came in January '92 from the engineering department at North Carolina A&T. He had a PhD from Stanford University, was young and aggressive, and set his sights on bringing prominence to PV's College of Engineering.

Not only was Carolyne responsible for student recruitment and the summer bridge program, but Dr. Foster expanded her responsibilities to include corporate and government relations. Carolyne was a good public relations person, and no one else in the college could commit to that function. During a period of reorganization, Dean Foster made the case to Academic Affairs that the College of Applied Sciences and Engineering Technology should be merged with the College of Engineering. His vision was that all engineering disciplines—pure engineering, engineering technology, and computer science (considered a companion course of study to engineering)—should be in the same college. This move opened new avenues for all engineering and engineering-related programs, especially computer science.

Carolyne and Dr. Foster were an awesome team as they built partnerships and brought more corporate and government support to all programs in the engineering college. Their plan of action to recruit corporate partners was interesting. Carolyne would research and scout out different companies, seek mutual engineering or computer science opportunities, and look for alumni who were employed with the companies to help build relationships. She was on the move, especially in the Dallas area, where many of our graduates were employed with technical companies. Once Carolyne got into a company, engaged the senior engineering or technical managers, and made her presentation of Prairie View and the College of Engineering, they would be on board to visit the campus. She made presentations to such companies as Tellabs in Chicago, McDonnell Douglas in Kansas City, Texas Instruments (TI), and Nortel Network Systems in the Dallas area, giving companies an opportunity to build a partnership with an HBCU to help meet their diversity requirements. Once the corporate representatives came to the campus, the visits would include tours of labs and departments, lunch, presentations by the dean and department heads, and discussion on future collaboration. We would be on our way to forging a partnership.

That strategy brought two major companies to computer science—Nortel Network Systems and Texas Instruments (TI). Although TI was already partnering with engineering, they were now open to partnering with computer science. Nortel, on the other hand, was a different situation. Ralphael Wilson, one of the early CS graduates, was employed with Nortel and took the lead in building the relationship on the corporate side. An entire computer laboratory was funded by Nortel Networks with Ralphael's involvement. He ensured that all of the equipment—our first Smart board, computers, student desks, carpet on the floor, as well as the services of technicians to install the lab—was donated. All we had to do was provide the space. Of course, TI was not going to allow Nortel to have greater exposure. So, Dr. Marvin Cowan, a supportive TI partner who was not a PV graduate, was successful in getting our second lab funded—computers, desks, chairs, and other equipment. Our students benefitted greatly from these new labs, exposing them to new technology.

The merger of computer science with engineering also meant the name of the summer bridge program would change. Engineering Concepts Institute became the Engineering and Science Concepts Institute (ESCI)—to include computer science. Engineering and computer science students were being recruited to the program. Carolyne was all over the state of Texas and out of state to cities such as Detroit, Chicago, and Los Angeles talking to students. She and Dean Foster created such excitement about ESCI that students were skipping their high school graduation ceremonies to come to Prairie View to enroll for the summer. This early start meant that many students were screened early and put on track for internships with corporate entities, a major draw to expose our program and engineering to interested high school students.

Carolyne worked with national student-focused organizations such as the National Society for Black Engineers (NSBE). The annual conferences shined a spotlight on our programs to students at other universities and to corporations. When the NSBE Conference was held in Houston in 1993, Dr. Foster, the engineering dean, wanted as much exposure as possible to the PV engineering and computer science programs. He wanted the college booth set on the exhibit hall floor with the corporate booths—some 350 or so major corporations—rather than in the designated section with other college booths. Carolyne took on the task of making this happen and ensured the college booth would stand out among the corporate booths. That was a bold move, but their gamble worked! From that point on, Prairie View's booth remained in the corporate section of the exhibit hall—no matter where the NSBE Conference was held.

Corporations paid attention! Carolyne had the students go to the corporate booths and invite representatives to stop by the PV booth for more information and schedule campus visits. This gave students the opportunity to improve their communication skills and develop relationships that often led to internships and jobs after graduation. Students at other universities were transferring to PV for engineering and computer science as news spread about internship opportunities and high-paying, post-graduate careers. Enrollment in computer science grew exponentially during that time. Companies remained interested in PV because of the number of minority engineering and computer science students and the quality of our programs. Corporations could fulfill their diversity requirements with ease with graduates who were well prepared to positively impact their organizations.

Carolyne became director of development for the university in 1995 and expanded what was known as the university's Cluster—a corporate partnership program that also existed on several other HBCU campuses. Engineering and computer science benefitted greatly from corporate partnerships through the program. She created *Cluster Magazine*, an annual publication that showcased corporate and university partnerships. The cover of the magazine featured PV's Cluster Company of the Year, a company that offered major support to the university for that year. Stories touted corporate funding through building labs and academic programs, faculty support, internship programs, and permanent hires. PV's Cluster received recognition from Southern Association of Colleges and Schools (SACS) during its 1998 university accreditation visit. Companies appreciated that level of recognition and continued to support our programs. The stellar performance of our students, once they entered the corporate world, further strengthened our relationships.

Software Engineering Initiative

As we continued to build corporate relationships and the academic strength of our students, NASA became a major player in the fall of 1997 by entering into a cooperative agreement to develop computer software engineering capability for the International Space Station (ISS) and the Space Shuttle Program. I was very familiar with this program because I worked on the first space shuttle, *Columbia*, when I was at Singer-Link. I was excited about partnering with NASA and reconnecting to the program. This was an unsolicited project called the Software Engineering Initiative (SEI). Ken Martindale from NASA Science, and who was with NASA when I worked at Lockheed, was the person who contacted me to lead this project.

We were awarded $895,596 over two years to build computer software engineering capability at Historically Black Colleges and Universities (HBCUs) and other Minority Institutions (MIs) for the International Space Station. The initiative was so successful, the Computer Science department was awarded $1.7 million for three more years, creating a five-year initiative for developing and implementing engineering software.

The initiative was developed in phases. In the first year, Phase 1, we developed the software core capability. This meant creating the curriculum, introductory software application projects (SAPs), and the internship program, as well as identifying interest groups and distance learning resources. Phase 2 (year 2) involved conducting core capability tests and demonstrations, enhancing and refining the curriculum, developing advanced SAPs, and enhancing the internship program and distance learning.

The next three years of funding were used to implement Phases 3, 4, and 5, which continued to show verification and readiness of the core capabilities through enhancing the curriculum, initiating advanced SAPs, continuing internship enhancement, and demonstrating capability applications, plus expanding the program to other HBCUs and MIs. Additionally, the goals of Phase 4 and 5 were to acquire and conduct funded research projects, continue introductory and advanced curriculum, create advanced SAPs, and strengthen the SEI.

This was a great opportunity for the computer science department and for the university. I was the principal investigator (PI) and handled project development, while Dr. G-Wahid, one of the computer science professors, took care of project implementation. We met a major collaborative goal by building a pipeline of graduates who had the requisite skills to support the software engineering needs of NASA and its aerospace companies.

The first group of PV students to intern at various companies in the NASA complex as a result of this collaboration were called the 'Elite Eight', a name given to them by the NASA team. The group included seven computer science students and one engineering student. We got even more exposure when the SEI partnership with NASA and the 'Elite Eight' students — Cedric Wilson, Kevin Holland, Eldridge Raymond, Jr., Orenthial Stevenson, Tara White, Caterina Charles, Diana Bell, and Angela Harrison, were featured in the university's Cluster magazine.

While at NASA in the summer of 1998, PV students completed software projects to train astronauts, attended lectures and seminars delivered by corporate professionals that immersed them in the corporate world, and were given NASA suits they could wear for photos. The students received an outstanding performance rating and raised the expectations of students coming from the PVAMU Computer Science Department. The following year, our intern cohort soared to twenty-one students. Many of them are in their forties now and are still working at NASA.

Cedric Wilson was a top student in our department and the leader of the 'Elite Eight' team. He and his family are members of our church. I had the opportunity to watch him grow as a person, earn his computer science degree, and go to work for NASA, like so many other students who were a part of the program. Cedric excelled in his profession, and I saw him get married, have children, and become a deacon at our church. It seems the foundation and experience Cedric received as one of the Elite Eight have served him well. It is rewarding to see students excel in their careers and in life.

We received a lot of publicity about the software initiative. The number of corporate and academic partners increased as the number of students in the program grew. Prairie View was now partnering with Texas A&M-Kingsville, GHG Corporation, and Smith Research Corporation (SRC). Nortel partnered with us in launching a Distance Learning Program with Texas A&M-Kingsville through an electronic interface to offer software engineering courses. Dr. Barbara Schreur, from Texas A&M-Kingsville, taught software engineering, and PV offered a Computer Organization class. Students were physically at Prairie View but were taught by the Kingsville professor, and Kingsville students were taught by a professor from Prairie View. These were the early stages of online education for the university.

The Nortel lab was a great teaching tool and allowed access to information via Interactive Distance Learning (IDL) technology, opening a world of increased learning opportunities with other HBCUs and MIs. All student assignments were online, and tests were offered online. It was called the "teaching tool of the future."

Another opportunity to promote the SEI was through the

Association of Computer/Information Sciences and Engineering Departments at Minority Institutions (ADMI) conference held in Houston in June 1998. ADMI was founded in August 1989 as a national organization dedicated to exploring and providing remedies to the educational issues in computer/information science and computer engineering that confront minority institutions of higher education. I joined ADMI as the Prairie View representative in 1993 and became a board member during my tenure with the organization. The Houston conference gave me an opportunity to present the Software Engineering Initiative to other HBCUs to solicit their participation and increase the HBCU partnership component. Hampton and Alabama A&M were ready to become involved. This consortium created the partnership that NASA was looking for—small businesses (GHG Corporation and SRC), MIs (Texas A&M-Kingsville), and HBCUs (Prairie View, Hampton University, and Alabama A&M).

The five-year Software Engineering Initiative plan was to produce a pipeline of skilled graduates in the software engineering discipline to support NASA's ISS (International Space Station) program. The university's small business program, the government, and its contractors were all involved in software engineering. SEI donated aerospace software and helped develop a teaching curriculum for Black colleges and technical institutions. We developed an aerospace software application project, including application demonstrations and research activities. All of this led to an understanding of software principles supporting desired skills in engineering.

Our students were proud of their education at PV, which allowed them to have great careers and recognition at their respective companies. Many chose to give back to the university by encouraging their companies to support their alma mater. This level of gratitude and philanthropy was of tremendous benefit to the computer science department and students at Prairie View.

By 2000, the Computer Science Department was progressing

full speed ahead. Our faculty was solid and working well together. I had stepped down from leading the department because I did not have a PhD. Dr. Yonggao Yang, one of the faculty members, was named department chair. Myrtle Thompkins and I paired up to teach Introduction to Computer Science, although I continued to seek partnership and funding opportunities. Ms. Thompkins took the lead in building and rolling out the Intro course that became part of the core curriculum for all PV students. The upper-level CS courses were being taught by Dr. Yang, Professor Ravi, Dr. Safwat Shakir, and Dr. Lin Li.

Our enrollment numbers were climbing steadily, and students were performing well in the curriculum. Some graduates went on to earn their master's and doctorate degrees in computer science or related fields at major universities across the nation. We had a good relationship with corporate and government agencies, and were still making progress with the Software Engineering Initiative.

The Storefront

Around this time, I received a call from Linda Flowers, manager of Lockheed Martin Mission Services (LMMS) Civil Programs. [The Lockheed Corporation, parent company of Lockheed Electronics, merged with Martin Marietta in March 1995 to become Lockheed Martin.] This component of Lockheed Martin was a major support contractor to NASA's Johnson Space Center through its Consolidated Space Operations Contract (CSOC). Flowers wanted to discuss an innovative program called the Storefront for educational outreach and support to meet NASA's goal of directing 1 percent of all prime and subcontractor funding to support HBCUs and MEIs (Minority Educational Institutions). The Storefront would be housed in a facility located on or near a university campus. Students would be employed on a part-time basis to perform engineering work for Lockheed Martin under the mentorship of Lockheed or subcontractor personnel. The storefronts would be viewed as an extension of Lockheed's workforce but located in a university community, and would provide real-world corporate experience for the students. The program would generate significant savings to NASA in software sustainment as a result of lower labor costs and expose students to opportunities available in the aerospace industry. Prairie View would be the first university targeted for this pilot program, and University of Texas at El Paso (MEI) was in line as the next site.

Flowers asked to schedule a meeting at her Lockheed office, and I could not have been more excited. I did not know if this opportunity was due to NASA and its subcontractors having experienced the quality of our students around the Software Engineering Initiative or because of my prior relationship with Lockheed. My employment at Lockheed Electronics at the Johnson Space Center spanned a period of ten years—1969–79. All the Lockheed mergers happened after I left the company. And here I was—back at Lockheed Martin—discussing an opportunity for the computer science and engineering students at Prairie View. I felt I had come full circle.

I contacted Bob Effinger, director of the Prairie View A&M Research Foundation (an extension of the Texas A&M Research Foundation), to relay my conversation with Flowers. He agreed that we should set a follow-up meeting. Bob, his assistant Darla, and I went to Clear Lake to meet with Flowers to discuss details regarding the project. We had a very productive meeting and left excited about the possibilities that existed for Prairie View. Following the meeting, Bob, Darla, and I went to the Kemah Boardwalk, had lunch, and discussed our next steps to embrace the opportunity presented to us. When I returned to campus, I sent an email to Dr. Willie Trotty, vice president of Research and Development, detailing both meetings and to make more definitive plans for follow-up meetings. He, too, was excited about the opportunities that might materialize from this partnership.

Lockheed Martin was a government contractor, and as per university policy, all funds from partnerships, proposals, and grants from local, state, and federal government agencies and entities had to be processed through the University's Research and Development Office and PV's Research Foundation. Dr. Trotty and Bob worked out details for direct and indirect costs, how project funds would be managed, and how the paperwork would be processed for the project. I got busy figuring out where the Storefront program would be housed and the process for getting students interested and involved.

After looking at various off-campus facilities, it was determined there wasn't a site with an Internet line (T1 line) capable of transmitting between the city of Prairie View and Lockheed Martin. I then began looking for an on-campus facility to house the project. The only on-campus stand-alone facility that I thought might work was Farrell Hall. The university's student computer center was located there, and before that, Farrell Hall was the student laundromat. After a conversation with the director of the computer center, I learned that it was being moved to the university library, leaving Farrell Hall vacant. Perfect!

I began figuring how to make Farrell Hall work. The university was going to have to do quite a bit of work to get the space ready—air-conditioning, painting, plumbing—a complete buildout to meet the specifications required by Lockheed. Most of the initial funds allocated were spent on the project start-up. The biggest priority was running a T1 line from the university library to Farrell Hall. The connection between Farrell Hall and Lockheed was critical so students could log on and have a direct connection to Lockheed. The T1 line cost showed up monthly on the Computer Science Department's phone bill. It was expensive, but worth every penny.

Lockheed Martin wanted to have a permanent facility on Prairie View's campus. The initial funding of $1 million was awarded to set up a dedicated space and launch the first phase of the Storefront project. Another partner involved in the program was Cimarron Software Services, Inc.—a woman-owned small business subcontractor. They handled hiring students, security clearances, drug testing, and managed the students who worked in the Storefront. GHG Corporation was another subcontractor—a disabled veteran, minority-owned business that provided the operation's engineering, quality assurance, and IT solutions.

Once Farrell Hall was operational and set up to resemble the Lockheed work environment—including the Lockheed Martin logo and specialty signage—we held a ribbon cutting ceremony on September 6, 2001. Senior administrators from both NASA and Lockheed were there to launch the Storefront, including George Abbey, Sr., former director of the Johnson Space Center; Doug Tighe, CSOS program manager; Roz Doyle, CEO of Cimarron; and Jay Honeycutt, president, Lockheed Martin Space Operations. Dr. Charles Hines, sixth president of Prairie View, was also present for the ceremony. That was a landmark day for the computer science department and the university!

As the program's principal investigator, I had the responsibility of managing university involvement in the Storefront. I recruited students and ensured they met all requirements on the university side to work at the facility. I also had oversight of the funding designated for the program.

Recruiting students to work in the Storefront program was not difficult. We posted flyers and advertised to get students who were computer science, information technology, or engineering majors to apply. They had to be U.S. citizens or green-card holders, meet the qualifications of being "full-time students in good standing" based on university requirements, maintain a minimum 2.75 GPA, and obtain three recommendations from faculty. Once the students qualified, they had to meet Lockheed employment requirements: pass a criminal background check and drug testing, submit to an interview with Lockheed representatives, and qualify for Lockheed Martin security clearance with company-generated identification/badging and Storefront access.

After students were hired to work, management was provided on several levels by Cimarron. The Storefront administrative manager would coordinate with Lockheed Martin on task assignments, schedules, and deliverables. The technical manager was the day-to-day mentor and coordinated aspects of the student employees' work that consisted of engineering tasks within the LMSO Engineering organization supporting the Johnson Space Center Mission Support Operations Contract (MSOC). Students did maintenance and modification of the Integrated Planning System and Mission Control Center operational software baseline; they developed and maintained the LM MSOC, designed and maintained the Storefront webpages, and updated and maintained AutoCAD drawings of the Mission Control Center.

Students who participated in this program gained knowledge that could not be obtained from a college textbook or classroom. Without leaving the campus they gained real work experience which gave them increased advantages when seeking employment. This gave employers access to graduates with real-world software engineering experience.

KC135 Initiative

With the Storefront project up and operational, we had another opportunity to work with NASA in 2002 in the KC135 Reduced Gravity Student Flight Opportunities Program. Willie Williams, another NASA representative, was assigned to us to work with students and guide them through the process. Teams of undergraduate students would generate ideas for microgravity experiments. They would develop their ideas through writing proposals, designing and building the experiments, and flying them on NASA's microgravity aircraft (the KC135). After the flight, students would share their experiences with a broader audience.

We formed four teams of students to consider four possible areas of submission—animal research, propellant research, radiation research, and variations of water spray patterns due to changes in nozzle size and reduced gravity. NASA announced in December 2003 that our water spray patterns experiment had been selected. Warren Hough was the lead student on this project, and he and his team could not have been more excited. This experiment was among the first to be chosen from an HBCU. There were seventy-one total experiments selected from over 100 proposals submitted in 2002. The Prairie View experiment was scheduled to fly in group five for the flight week in July 2003. I was excited for the students and knew that they would do well. Students found the experience rewarding because they had an opportunity to take an idea from conception to implementation and to experience microgravity work. What an awesome opportunity. I was proud for them!

Our department continued its outreach program that began in the late '80s to middle and high school students. Among the early groups was the Wheeler Avenue Baptist Church Boy Scout Troop that came for a computer introduction workshop and to learn about our computer science department. We worked with James Clark, a deacon of the church and Scout Master, to arrange the workshop. I was excited about having the boys from our church visit the campus and thrilled because our son, Jay, was a part of the group. It was important to me that he would see his dad in action! After the SEI was up and running in the late 90s, Pearl Wright, one of our advisory board members, worked with us to partner with Sterling High School in the Houston Independent School District (HISD). Sterling was known for its aviation program, and we saw this as an opportunity to introduce those students to Prairie View, our department, and our partnership with NASA and the SEI program.

We did an assessment in 2013 of the Storefront program and were amazed at its accomplishments. Over 100 students had worked at the PVAMU Storefront since its inception in 2001. Many were employed with Lockheed Martin or Cimarron as systems engineers, performance engineers, operating systems engineers, software engineers, and security engineers. Graduates worked at Lockheed Martin and Cimarron locations across the country, including Houston, Fort Worth, Denver, and Washington, DC. Some went to work for other companies such as United Space Alliance, Raytheon, Exxon Mobil, Accenture, Chicago Bridge & Iron, and the Central Intelligence Agency (CIA).

When Johnson Space Center administrators were looking for young people with the right training, connection, and interaction, they looked for students who were part of the Storefront program. These students already had security clearance and were in the pipeline to be hired. When PV students were hired after graduation to work at either Johnson Space Center or Lockheed Martin, they would be working with some of the same supervisors who had mentored and guided them through the process, and they would have already been assimilated into that work environment. The Storefront was the only program of its kind in the United States.

Sometimes we had a hard time placing our students with NASA for permanent hire. It was a government agency with government salaries and couldn't compete with the private sector. Students would go to NASA for the co-op/internship, and the agency wanted to hire them, but they couldn't offer competitive pay. A student had to be dedicated to the aerospace program and the prestige of working for NASA to stay with the agency. A number of our students also did not pursue advanced degrees immediately after graduation, or pursued them later, because they could go into private industry and earn major salaries.

After working on the Software Engineering Initiative, the

Storefront was the logical next step. My focus was to get the Storefront up and running to expose our students to the aerospace industry. I was satisfied with the project. It evolved at a good pace and I wouldn't have done anything differently. I had strong support from the industry and university administrators. The industry involvement really brought that program along, and their support came at just the right time.

The Storefront was the campus jewel. One could walk into Farrell Hall and it was "wow"—a corporate work environment on campus. The Storefront program yielded $15 million to Prairie View in the thirteen years I managed the project. I felt good about the outcome of the program. It was a signature project that I believe was ahead of its time.

Teaching and Tenure

I still had a full teaching load in addition to building the computer science program and department, getting accreditation, recruiting students, and getting continuous funding. I taught two days of the week and managed projects and sought funding the other three days. There were fewer students in early classes, but in later years, when I taught Intro to Computer Education, I would have about forty students in each of three classes each semester.

When I taught sophomore and upper-level courses such as Assembly Language, Simulation and Modeling, and Ethics, the maximum number of students enrolled would be fifteen or twenty. I had graduate assistants to grade papers, because I had little time for that due to handling administrative duties. Classrooms were large enough to hold forty computer stations, but when I taught upper-level or advanced classes, there were more terminals than students, due to the limited number of students who pursued computer science as a major. My teaching tools also changed over the time. In the early years, I used slides and other visuals to support my lectures, but later moved to PowerPoint.

The desks in the classrooms had a keyboard and a monitor on the top, and the hard drive was under the desk. Sometimes the students would bring their own laptops, especially since they likely had the latest computer upgrades on their personal devices. The university was behind in installing upgrades since everything happened so fast in the industry. There was only one printer in the room, usually in a corner, but all computers were connected to it. If the students sent something over, they would have to wait a little while to get their printouts.

I remained in academics because I enjoyed teaching and there was more time off—two weeks at Christmas, plus the spring and summer breaks. I could take a vacation and spend time with family—even though Carolyne insisted I never took enough time off to rest or to be with family. I was a twelve-month associate professor—never a full professor because I did not have a PhD. So, I would go into the office in the summer but did not teach, giving me even more time to manage projects, research opportunities to continue to grow the program, and prepare for the coming academic year.

When I was hired to build the Computer Science program at Prairie View, I was put on tenure track for the required six years. I went through the whole process and earned an associate professorship in 1988. When on a tenure track, you have to conduct research, publish papers, attend and present at conferences, incur service hours, and so forth. The university looked at your teaching record, the number of students who matriculated through your curriculum, and the number of committees on which you served.

Service hours came from working on committees. There were committees for promotion and tenure, scholarship, faculty search, post-tenure review, accreditation, and the undergraduate computer science program—about eight total. I was going to committee meetings regularly. We would have to meet and assist professors who were on tenure track, review their work, and evaluate them.

Young professors could get tenured at Prairie View. Once they acquired tenure, some would leave to accept higher-paying positions at a major institution. But many would stay, and I hired some of them in the Computer Science department. It was difficult to hire African Americans. They were sought after because major universities were seeking to diversify their faculty and offered better pay.

Professors had to present at a certain number of conferences—at least three each year. Every year, I went to the ACM and ADMI conferences, which rotated to different colleges and cities. I would write and present a paper, then the body would publish it in a journal—that took care of my publication record. We would also attend conferences to make connections with professors we would consider for positions in our program at Prairie View. ACM was good for learning new trends in the industry, and I presented the Software Engineering Initiative there. It took me several months to write the paper, working part time on research and writing and building the slides to put on the overhead projectors for the presentation (that was long before PowerPoint).

All the long hours and work were worth it because most of our students had jobs the day they received their degrees. The thought of a student going through four years of college and not able to find a job upon graduation was frustrating to me. It seemed almost like a waste of time. But every student who graduated in computer science had one or multiple job offers. Recruiters would come to campus, and CS students could almost pick and choose jobs—that was the value of the program. We had a high placement rate for our graduates, including employment at Fortune 500 companies and major corporations around the country. The only negative was that we had small graduating classes. Our students were well prepared, but there were not enough of them. Our program was quite challenging, and we oftentimes had a problem with retention. Sometimes students couldn't commit; they couldn't handle the rigor and most of the mathematics.

Computer science was structured, so some students struggled a bit. We offered tutoring, but some still didn't make it through.

Generally, we had more women than men in the program, and that remained true most of the time I was there. The women worked harder than the men, and they were more determined. The men got caught up in fraternities and sports, and that caused some of them to drop out. I have to give it to the women. They hung tough. There was never a problem with discipline in the classroom or anything like that, not with those majors. They wanted to learn the material and go into industry to earn a good income. It's a rough estimate, but perhaps 400-500 students graduated in computer science the thirty-two years I was teaching.

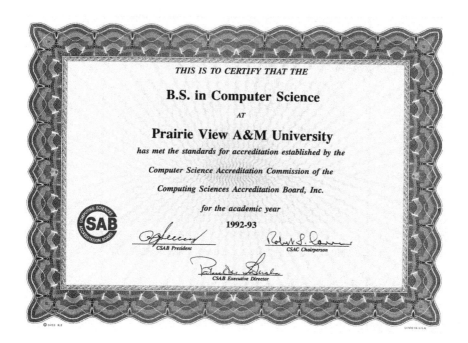

THIS IS TO CERTIFY THAT THE

B.S. in Computer Science

AT

Prairie View A&M University

has met the standards for accreditation established by the

Computer Science Accreditation Commission of the

Computing Sciences Accreditation Board, Inc.

for the academic year

1992-93

CSAB President

CSAC Chairperson

CSAB Executive Director

CSAB Accreditation Certificate for Computer
Science at Prairie View – 1992-93
(Author Collection)

134

Brochure promoting the Lockheed Martin
Storefront program at Prairie View.
(Author Collection)

Elite 8 – First students to intern as part of the Software
Engineering Initiative with NASA – 1998 (Author Collection)

Chapter 8

Prairie View Today

Prairie View A&M University is one of the most beautiful campuses in the country today. It looks nothing like the campus my brother and I set foot on as undergraduate students back in 1957. When A.D. returned with me to the campus in 2011 to celebrate our 50th class reunion, he was amazed at how much the campus had changed.

Our reunion brought back memories as we greeted our classmates and their spouses. It was good to reflect on days gone by, but what was especially rewarding was catching up on the events of our lives and seeing those classmates whom we had not seen since our graduation 50 years ago.

We felt special that year when our class was recognized at spring commencement and our reunion luncheon. In the fall, we were the guests of honor at Homecoming. We received special attention at the parade, at the football game where our class made a large gift to the university, and later that evening at our reunion gala. Everyone reflected on how the campus had changed and how so much more had been added to the campus. But despite all the changes, the remaining

100-year-old oak trees still gave the campus a stately feel.

Carolyne and I drove through the campus not long ago and were amazed at the growth. I like to stop by and take a look whenever we are traveling that way. What is most impressive is the new student housing for undergraduates, and now separate housing for graduate and married students. Nothing like what A.D., Paul Stiner, and I lived in when we were there. There are new classroom buildings, brick building identification signs to help with directions, new parking lots, student parks, the new football stadium - I am happy to have been a financial supporter - and the new clock tower that reminds me of the old campus. Strip shopping centers are being built around the campus to offer retail services to students. Prairie View is beginning to look like a "college town."

Most impressive is the new welcome center that overlooks a man-made lake. The view made me proud to be an alumnus—what an awesome image! The lake is located on what was an open field at the front of the campus. In the late 1990s and early 2000s when Carolyne was there as development director, an alumni wall park was in that space, displaying the bricks and pavers purchased by those who wanted to support scholarships at PV.

I am so inspired by what Dr. Ruth Simmons, the current president, is doing and the life she is breathing into the campus. Prairie View is realizing its full potential, and a great vision seems to be coming to fruition. I believe the academic programs are strong, made obvious by the increased enrollment in computer science and engineering. Many of the professors with whom I worked are retired now, but I know that Prairie View's Computer Science curriculum is still a strong program. There's no question about it. I visited the Computer Science website recently, and my heart was filled with joy when I saw all the department is doing. The faculty has grown and there is continued corporate involvement, especially with companies like Google and Intel.

Academic legacy

Teaching is a call to knowledge. My philosophy was, and still is, the belief that everything I did required students to be engaged in the learning process. I worked to pique students' interest and help them gain skills in such a way that they could apply and transfer the knowledge they learned in a classroom setting to their professional work environment.

These goals guided the way I prepared and presented materials in class and tested students. I used homework assignments requiring critical thinking and problem-solving skills. I developed and presented examples in my lectures. I asked transfer questions that tested students' ability to apply what they learned in one context to another.

I taught because I enjoyed it, and because of the need as instilled in me by my aunt Callie. I taught because I believed teaching is learning. Much of my passion for teaching came from my expectation that others should be as driven to learn as I was. Learning was fun for me, and much of my teaching style came from my own observations of how I was best able to learn. Enthusiasm for acquiring knowledge is contagious, and if I could show excitement for a subject, those I taught were more likely to focus their attention and remember. Learning requires an exchange between teacher and student that is respectful and not distant. I always strived to provide a friendly, professional environment that emphasized knowledge and improvement. Making mistakes is an expected and unavoidable process of learning. I had high expectations for my students. I saw more value in encouraging a student to meet a goal. I read once that learning is not a spectator sport. Active participation and relating the topic to personal experience and interest are crucial to success in the classroom.

I believe that teachers must be communicators of intellectual honesty, academic integrity, fairness, dignity, and trust in every aspect of their instruction, maybe in every aspect of their lives, because one cannot teach these values without living them.

140

J.D. and A. D. at their 50th Class Reunion
Prairie View A&M University – 2011
(Author Collection)

Prairie View A&M University Campus
(Prairie View A&M University Website)

College of Juvenile Justice and Psychology Building
Prairie View A&M University (Author Collection)

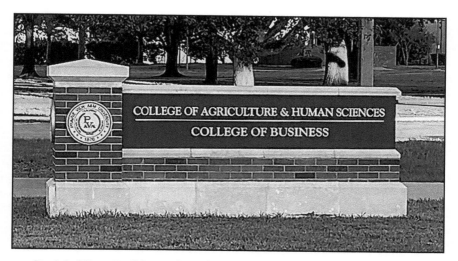

Prairie View Building Identification Signage (Author Collection)

Panther Football Stadium on the campus of Prairie View
- Opened in 2016 (Author Collection)

EPILOGUE

146 A Heart of Giving

In 2019, NASA celebrated the 50th anniversary of the lunar landing. What a historic moment! NASA made history again that year when two women stepped out into space. It is good to be around to celebrate and witness history in the making. An awesome feeling! Also, there's the return of the five-year module from Jupiter. That's exciting, the moons orbiting Jupiter. There have been renditions done and some blurry looks through telescopes, but humans never witnessed the moons' actual orbit. And those moons were moving pretty fast.

I try to keep up with what's going on with the space program. I read the paper and I'm glad to see that the space program is still being supported. It has been about three years since I have been out to the Johnson Space Center, but I didn't see a lot of change the last time I went, other than the fact that fewer people are working there. Being there brought back a lot of memories. Lockheed Martin signage is still at the building where I worked, but the building is empty. The NASA complex is the same size, but they have concentrated staff into a smaller area.

When astronaut Scott Kelly lived in the International Space Station for a year to assess what long-term effects of living in space would have on the body, I was especially interested and related to that flight. He, too, has an identical twin brother, and I understand the project was designed to test how weightlessness affects two people who are alike in height and build. The results showed that when Kelly returned from space, his overall health was good, but he had grown two inches, then shrunk back to his normal height after a short period of time. Interesting stuff.

From what I read and hear, NASA is trying to prepare for manned flight to other planets such as Mars and Jupiter. Mars seems to be the primary project. Most of the space work is done by contractors, and just as in the earlier years, a lot of testing is being done to prepare to send man to Mars. It is too risky at this point. But I believe NASA is going to get there one day because the agency is again spending money on the space program. Space exploration always translates to a lot of spin-offs that benefit our society. Amazing. I would love to be a part of those teams now.

While some things in industry are still challenging for African Americans, I appreciate the opportunities my brother and I had. Lockheed Electronics and Singer-Link recognized me for the projects I worked on, and McDonnell Douglas recognized A.D. for his projects. I still have my certificates and that means a lot.

Family

My family has changed over the past few years. Jay, my niece, and all my nephews are adults. My brother Earl's two sons, Stephen and David, still live in New Jersey. Stephen attended Montclair State University, and David attended Yale. They both have an entrepreneurial spirit and own their own companies—much like their father and uncle, A.D. Stephen is in finance and David is in marketing. Stephen married and has three children—Hartlei, Stephanie, and Christopher. David is single with no children but spent much of his time caring for his father and his mom, Henrine. Earl, like our mother, had heart disease. He fought it for some time but lost his battle in July of 2016. His wife, Henrine, passed away in 2019.

My sister Gladys has three children. Trey (Leslie Chandler, III) is the oldest, is married, and has been working for the United States Department of Agriculture (USDA) as an animal health technician for more than twenty years. Livia, my only niece, worked as an agriculture instructor in public schools (Houston Independent School District) for a while, then went back to Prairie View, earned her counseling certification, and is now an academic counselor. She is married and has a daughter, Amanda Annette. The youngest is Eric, and he is the one who has come full circle. Growing up at home in Dime Box, he completed his undergraduate degree in agriculture at

Prairie View, then went on to Texas A&M University, where he received his PhD in Veterinary Medicine (DVM). He is a veterinarian, working mostly in west Texas, but still manages all the family land. He has his own herd of cows that he manages with his brother, Trey, and his father, Eddie Lee. My father hoped that his children or his grandchildren would follow the path he and my aunt Callie opened in education and land ownership. He is probably smiling now.

Our son, Jay, returned to Houston in 2005 from Hampton, Virginia. I had open heart surgery that year and I was happy to have him home. He went into the restaurant industry before he left Hampton, so he transferred to Houston with the same restaurant chain. After a few years in Houston, he became a manager at a well-known seafood restaurant and has settled in. I am so proud of the close relationship we have. He always calls to check in on us, and I just love my conversations with him. The three of us have gone on vacations together, and wherever we go—nationally or internationally—Jay is so patient with me and is always there to help. With my health challenges, Jay being there for us is such a relief for Carolyne and makes things a bit easier for the both of us.

My brother, A.D., passed away in May 2019. We were rarely apart, right until the end. God was merciful, but I miss him terribly. He had Parkinson's disease—was diagnosed a year or so before my diagnosis in 2009. He had a little more trouble managing the disease, but he kept reading scripture and praying. He served many years as a deacon at his church, Brentwood Baptist, so he continued to hold onto his faith. He and I had different journeys with Parkinson's. He became more reclusive and did not want to socialize much. I had hoped he would go to therapy or the exercise programs with me, walk with me, or just continue our visits, but he didn't, although we visited on the phone sometimes. Complications from the disease caused his demise.

Carolyne would have gatherings at our home for birthdays,

Christmas dinners, or "just because" get-togethers, and A.D. would come. In 2018, she invited friends and family over to celebrate our 80th birthdays. We had a beautiful time. Later that year, Jay and our nephew Kirk hosted Christmas dinner at our home—another great evening with family and friends I will never forget. That was the last time A.D. came to our home.

I was diagnosed with early-stage Parkinson's after Carolyne and I returned from summer vacation in 2009. We had gone to Palm Desert, California to relax and enjoy the beautiful golf courses. When we went bicycle riding, I kept falling off. I could not understand why I could not keep my legs moving to ride. That was something I knew how to do. I went to the doctor as soon as we returned and was diagnosed with the disease.

I tried to maintain a normal life the first years after the diagnosis. I thought it would be just a matter of taking medication as prescribed and having regular doctor's visits. However, as the disease progressed and I began to have side effects from the medication, I could see that my routine and stamina were being interrupted—concentration, sleep, speech. It was harder for me to get my words out. Another noticeable change was that my handwriting was getting smaller. This was a problem in teaching because I had to concentrate harder when writing on paper or on the chalkboard to ensure my handwriting was legible. Then I noticed I began to get stiff and had more difficulty walking. My movements became slower and slower—began to shuffle as I walked. I wasn't sure how I was going to handle this and continue to work, especially when I had to drive. By the time I arrived on campus, I was a bit tired from concentrating on driving. So, I would have to get there early enough to rest before classes. Oftentimes in the evenings after my workday, I would have to rest before driving back to Houston.

After I got dizzy and fell a few times before going to work, Carolyne stepped in and decided to go to the doctor with me so she could understand what I was going through. She researched my medications and met with the doctor to be sure that I was on the right regimen. Carolyne was determined that we would manage this disease together. She retired in 2015 and got busy learning all she could about Parkinson's. She made sure I kept every doctor's appointment and followed through on every scheduled therapy session, monitored my medications to make sure I took everything on time, and managed my meals so that I ate properly. She got us involved with the Houston Area Parkinson's Society (HAPS) and its exercise program. Carolyne encouraged me to go every week, and after spending four years in the exercise programs—physical and voice, socialization and exercise through senior programs with local churches, walking and exercising at home—I feel we have learned to manage the disease. Even with all of that, there are some days I can hardly walk and some days I can walk and move with no assistance. Somedays I can hardly get my words out and some days my voice is strong. I try to remain as active and as independent as I can, knowing the day might come when I can do very little.

My doctor's reports are good now, and I feel good about myself. I don't know where I would have been if Carolyne had not stepped in. We try to get to Church every Sunday with a dinner outing afterward - a longstanding tradition with us. We go to Bible Study, visit family and friends in our hometowns, take short vacations, and sometimes we just get in the car and go for a ride.

We look forward to football season—watching professional and college ball. We like to keep up with the SEC—Texas A&M for me and for a while Carolyne favored Alabama, especially when their quarterback was Jalen Hurts, who is from Houston. Of course, I like to keep up with Prairie View and how they rank in SWAC (Southwest Athletic Conference). We also follow the Houston Texans and just wish they would win the Super Bowl! There are some great players on the team, especially Deshaun Watson.

Carolyne and I went to see the movie *Hidden Figures*—about the African American women who were mathematics analysts (referred to back then as human computers) at the Aeronautical Laboratory at Langley in Hampton, Virginia. That is an excellent movie. I didn't know anything about these ladies when I was at Lockheed. I interfaced with the chairman of the computer science department at Hampton when I was at Prairie View because I had the Software Engineering Initiative, but still wasn't aware of the contribution of the African American female analysts, especially Katherine Johnson, until I saw the movie being promoted on television. We have now seen it numerous times.

As I look back over my life, all I can say is "Thank you, Lord." When I think about where I came from and look at where I am now, I know the Lord has been good to me! I have been blessed with a loving family, caring friends, and reasonable health and strength. Although the Parkinson's disease can be challenging, I am just grateful to be where I am.

It was a long journey, but one that I would travel all over again if I had to.

J.D. standing alongside the old
Lockheed Martin Signage (offsite) – 2016
(Author Collection)

J.D. in front of Columbia Space Shuttle
replica at Space Center Houston – 2017
(Author Collection)

J.D. and A.D. at Family Christmas Gathering -
December 2018 (Author Collection)

Lightning Source UK Ltd.
Milton Keynes UK
UKHW022159190321
380669UK00010B/508/J